JOE DORIGO

CHARTWELL
BOOKS, INC.

A QUINTET BOOK

Published by Chartwell Books
A Division of Book Sales, Inc.
110 Enterprise Avenue
Secaucus, New Jersey 07094

ISBN 1-55521-788-5

This book was designed and produced by
Quintet Publishing Limited
6 Blundell Street
London N7 9BH

Creative Director: Richard Dewing
Designers: Ian Hunt, Stuart Walden
Project Editor: William Hemsley
Editor: Sam Merrell

Typeset in Great Britain by
Central Southern Typesetters, Eastbourne
Manufactured in Singapore by Eray Scan Pte Ltd
Printed in Singapore by
Star Standard Industries Private Ltd.

CONTENTS

WHAT IS THE MAFIA?

THE MAFIA IS, quite simply, a criminal organization that was in the right place at the right time. They have come a long way from the "buckwheat" killings of the 1920s and 1930s, when victims, such as Action Jackson, were horribly tortured to death as an example to anyone who might cross the Mob. Jackson was suspended naked by his feet from a meat-hook, beaten with a baseball bat, slashed with a razor, and had his eyes burned out with a blowtorch. He did not die of his wounds, but of shock, and, according to some sources, he took two days to die.

Today, the Mafia is at least as heavily involved in legitimate business as it is in extortion and prostitution. Their power, legitimate or otherwise,

is enormous. For instance, it has been seriously (and credibly) suggested that the assassination of John F. Kennedy was a Mafia hit job.

What then was the "right place at the time time"? After all, criminal organizations are nothing new. They existed in Ancient Rome and they can be found as tribal organizations in primitive societies today. To a large extent, the pirates of the Spanish Main were "organized crime"; they had conferences, respected one another's territories – and killed one another as necessary. As recently as the 1970s, a whole new cocaine-growing, manufacturing and dealing organization was founded, the much-feared and much-hated Medellin Cartel of Columbia.

"The right place" for the Mafia was the United States of America, and "the right time" was the beginning of Prohibition in the 1920s, which was a period when any determined, hard-working criminal could not only get ahead, but become a folk-hero into the bargain.

THE EMERGENCE
OF THE MAFIA

What brought the Mafia to the fore was that at that time the Italians were the most recent immigrants. They were therefore, by force of circumstance, the inhabitants of the squalid slums of America's mushrooming cities, such as New York and Chicago. Some of their children were what would today be called "streetwise" kids,

ABOVE
The courtyard of slum
buildings in the Italian
area of New York
around the beginning of
the 20th century.

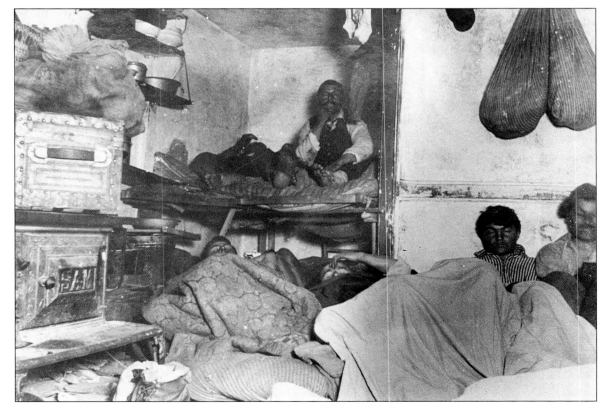

LEFT
Recent immigrants to the
United States in
unauthorized lodgings
in the 1890s. Although
the conditions in such
lodgings were
appalling, they were
somewhere cheap to
sleep for the night.

young punks brought up in the most appalling conditions who saw crime as the easiest or only way to "make good".

The Jews, fleeing the *Shtetls* of Eastern Europe, had been the previous wave. Accordingly, the previous generation of gang leaders (and some of the "goons", the "enforcers") had included a good number of Jews. Gang names now long forgotten, like the Monk Eastman gang, referred not to Italians but to Jews. Before them there had been the Irish. In the nineteenth century, it was the Irish gangs who struck terror into the hearts of law-abiding American citizens, gangs with names like the Dead Rabbits in New York, or the Bloody Tubs in Philadelphia. Like their successors, they were into extortion and "protection money". If payment was not made, one favoured trick was apparently to gouge out the victim's eyes. There were still plenty of Irish and Jewish bootleggers

around as the Sicilians came into power, and some had names like Kennedy and Annenberg.

Sociologists call this "ethnic succession in organized crime". Each new wave of immigrants lives first in the poorest parts of town. This spawns some violence and crime, but also a great deal of hard work and self-improvement. They then move up the social ladder, partly by their own efforts and partly by being displaced from below by yet another wave. In the 1970s and 1980s, a lot of noise was being made about Hispanic gangs, especially the Cubans in Florida and the Mexicans in California, who were the immigrants of the 1950s and 1960s. By the early 1990s, various Oriental gangs were just beginning to attract attention – especially the Japanese equivalent of the Mafia, the Yakuza. The Orientals accounted for the most recent wave of immigration in the 1980s and 1990s.

RIGHT
A few minutes after the start of Prohibition in a large New York cafe near Broadway, 1919. The bar has been stripped completely bare of any alcohol, and the customers have departed.

BELOW
The Latin American connection: drug traffickers killed in Central America in a gun battle with the police and army. These gang members were just one end of a wide network of organized crime that extends across continents into the United States.

THE PROFITS
OF PROHIBITION

What "froze" the Mafia in place, though, was principally the enormous opportunities for making staggering amounts of money in crimes that were substantially victimless – or where at least, the "victims" of bath-tub gin and rot-gut whiskey were far from complaining about their victimization. Anyone who delivered booze was, in popular eyes, not a criminal but a hero. There may have been millions of Americans who supported the dull, grey, rule-bound world that was implied by Prohibition; but they were not really the ones who counted. In business, in the media, in the arts, in high (or even middle) society and in politics, alcohol had for centuries been an essential social lubricant. The movers and shakers were not about to give up their drink, and as the movers and shakers included a good number of those who were in a position either to enforce or to ignore prohibition, enforcement was *not* the path they chose. In retrospect, there was no way Prohibition was ever going to work. One can only imagine that those who allowed Prohibition to pass into law were mentally crossing their fingers, and adding an invisible codicil that said, of course, it did not actually apply to *them*.

The third factor that made the word "Mafia" synonymous with organized crime was that the Sicilians had a long-established social and economic structure that included organized crime. Obviously, an organization must have a structure if it is going to survive; and now is the time to jump back across the centuries and look at the origins of the Mafia.

ABOVE
A group of men wearing straw "skimmers" having a last drink together before the start of Prohibition in 1919.

SICILIAN ROOTS

There is no doubt that the Maifa originally came from Sicily. Nor is there any doubt that Sicily has been home to criminal organizations for many centuries. For most of the country's history these organizations were the nearest that there was to effective government. Two things that are in doubt, though, are how the Mafia started, and whether the seven centuries of history that they claim is unbroken.

There are two main stories about the remote origins of *Mafia*. One says that it is an acronym deriving from *Morte alla Francia Italia anela!* ("Death to the French is Italy's cry!"), which refers to the long period when Sicily was dominated by the French Angevin dynasty. The other says that it refers to a rape which took place on Easter Monday, 1282. A French soldier (or several French soldiers) raped a Sicilian girl on her wedding day. The distraught mother ran through the streets screaming *"Ma fia! Ma fia!"* ("My daughter! My

daughter!"), and in the uprising that followed the original "Sicilian Vespers" of Easter Tuesday, 1282 thousands (or more likely hundreds) of Frenchmen were massacred.

Either way, there was undoubtedly a strong political component to the original Mafia. This is not unusual, because there have been many other societies that were either political or criminal, depending on whose side you were on. For instance, a contemporary of this original Mafia was the German *Vehm* or *Vehmgericht*. The Italian *Carbonari* of the eighteenth and nineteenth century, who had a major role in the unification and independence of Italy, also settled a few old scores and raised money by means of robber, intimidation and murder.

The difficulty, however, is that there is precious little to link the Mafia of medieval times with the Mafia of the nineteenth century. There were gangs in Sicily from 1300 to 1800, but they do not seem to have had much connection with anything we would recognize as "Mafia".

BELOW
An undated engraving shows the uprising that followed the original "Sicilian Vespers" of Easter Tuesday, 1282, in which large numbers of Frenchmen were massacred.

ORGANIZED CRIME IN ITALY

In Italy during the nineteenth century, two major centres of organized crime arose. One was Naples, home of the Camorra, and the other was Sicily, home of the Mafia. A third, almost as important, was Calabria in southern Italy, where a similar organization was known as the *Onorta Societa*, variously translated as the Honoured Society, the Honourable Society, and the Society of Honour. The Camorra was primarily urban, while the other two were primarily rural.

Yet a fourth group, but not truly organized at all, was the Black Hand. The Black Hand was never a gang, but a simple extortion racket where the victim was asked to pay up some money or face a variety of unpleasant consequences. These might range from a beating to the slaughter of cattle and the burning down of a house or even death. The "Black Hand" name came from the traditional way of presenting the demand. A letter was "signed" with the print of a hand dipped in black ink (a drawing of a hand replaced it as fingerprinting became widely used). Clearly, a few toughs or even a single bully-boy could issue "Black Hand" threats, and be reasonably sure of collecting. If several "Black Hand" extortionists were working in the same area, some of them might never resort to violence at all. They would rely on the fear generated by other, more dangerous "Black Handers" to get their money in.

Exactly what caused the rise of these groups or rackets is not, however, clear. The likeliest reason is simply opportunity. In a country in turmoil – a country that was not yet unified – there was plenty of opportunity for banditry. The rise in European living standards, due to the Industrial Revolution, also meant that the bandits had more to steal, and better technology to steal it with.

BELOW
Ignazio Saietta, a "Black Hander" who was known to the Italian community in New York that he terrorized as "Lupo the Wolf".

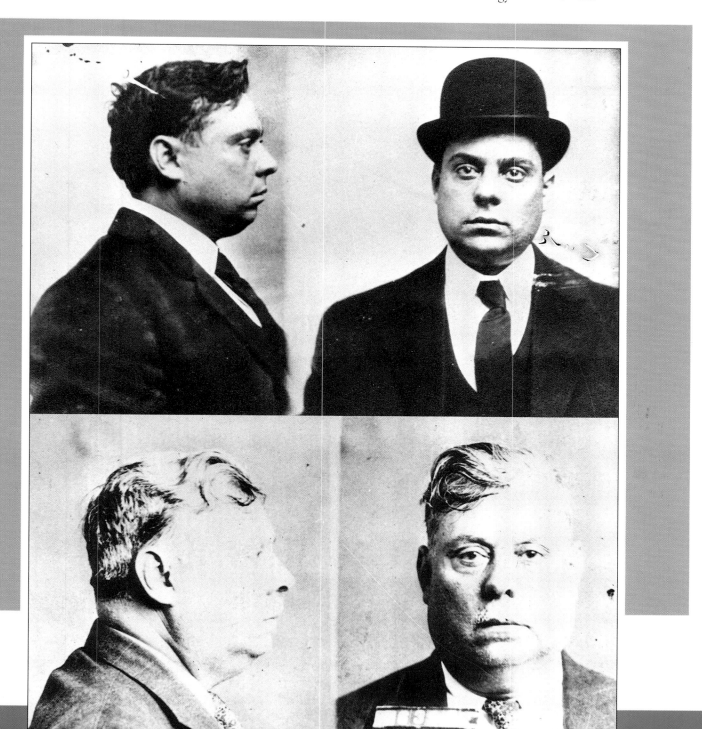

OMERTA

It also seems extremely likely that organized crime was overlaid upon (or merged with) the centuries-old tradition of the vendetta or blood feud. *Omertà*, "manliness", was an overdeveloped sense of honour, which existed especially in Sicily. It was the kind of "honour" that required a death to avenge an insult; a death that was in itself an insult, and which could only be avenged in one way and so it went on.

This sort of "honour" is easy to produce. Either you feed a man's ego until it can tolerate no affront, or you beat a man down until a quick temper and a willingness to lash out is all the honour that is left to him. In the former case you produce the medieval knight or the Prussian *Junker;* in the latter, you produce the gangster. In order to appease what remains of their consciences, either type of person will also produce all kinds of formal rules, which strictly define when they may or may not maim or kill. The knight adhered to the codes of chivalry, and the gangster develops a desperate attachment to the gang, because without it he is on his own. This is why *omertà* is often translated as the "code of silence".

Omertà created men who were ready to kill, and who were accustomed to killing. Organized crime created the need for killers, and it is easy to understand why.

In the legitimate world, there are all kinds of sanctions: fines, imprisonment, community service, even mere ridicule, as in the decision of some authorities to publish lists of whores' customers, or of fathers who do not pay child support. Legal sanctions do not usually extend to mutilation, torture and death, but they can and they have. Traitors (particularly regicides) were formerly tortured to death; thieves are mutilated to this day in fundamentalist Islamic societies; and the death penalty probably exists in more places than it is banned. That these penalties are imposed on criminals is irrelevant, but what is important is that they are imposed legitimately. The monopoly of violence by the state is the fundamental underpinning of any half-way stable society.

In criminal life, by contrast, most non-violent sanctions are simply not available. In many countries, even where gambling is legal, gambling debts are not legally enforceable: they are merely "debts of honour". If you are running a gambling chain and someone refuses to pay, you cannot sue them. If someone is skimming your profits, you may be able to bring a suit if gambling is legal, but if it is not the only thing you are able to do is put the frighteners on him.

BELOW
Omertà: a code of honour that leads to killing and yet more killing. Here the police cover up the body of yet another victim of a Mafia "hit" as it lies on the street in midtown Manhattan.

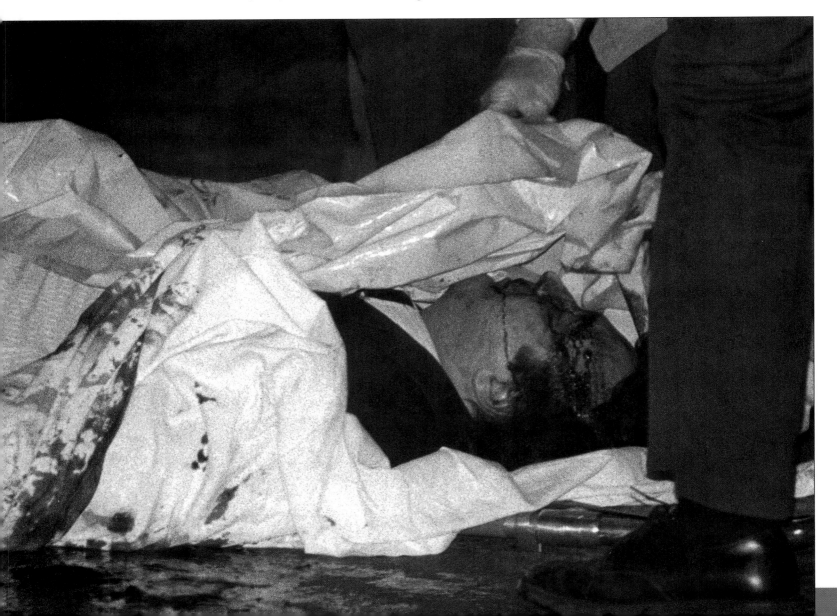

THE LAND OF OPPORTUNITY

By the middle of the nineteenth century, therefore, there existed in Sicily a "parallel" government that lacked only one thing: the opportunity to make a *lot* of money. There were plenty of opportunities for petty crime, it was true, such as protection money from small businesses, "numbers games" (illegal lotteries), minor-league confidence tricks, and cattle theft. It was possible to do a little better out of prostitution, provided you controlled enough girls, but for a mafioso this would probably offend against *omertà*. The occasional kidnapping could make a lot more money, but there just was not a large enough reservoir of potential victims, and few people could afford really significant ransoms. With a relatively small, poor population on a relatively small, poor island, the Mafia was limited in what it could do. The opportunities for the Camorra were somewhat greater, which may have been why the Camorra was slightly less horribly violent than the Mafia. For example, a camorrista would traditionally slit an informer's tongue before killing him, so that those who found the body would know why he had died; but a mafioso would cut off his genitals, ram them down his throat, and then kill him.

The United States, of course, was the Land of Opportunity at least as much for criminals as for honest people. With a bigger population in a vast country where wealth was all but waiting to be picked up, the spoils for the successful criminal were very much greater, and that was just from the point of view of traditional crime. The United States presented completely new opportunities, with possibilities that were practically limitless. Three of the biggest supporters of organized crime in the United States in the late-nineteenth and early twentieth centuries were politicians, big business and organized labour.

POLITICS BUSINESS AND UNIONS

Politicians, especially in relentlessly corrupt Chicago, found that it was cheaper and easier to buy gangland "minders" than it was to buy the voters themselves. The "minders" went along to the polls, and with the aid of blackjacks and revolvers simply terrorized the voters into voting for the correct candidate. This method of coercion continued well into the twentieth century. The so-called "Pineapple Primary" of 1928 took its name from the way that armed gangs used bombs

(nicknamed "pineapples") to suport their faction in the Chicago Republican Party primary. For decades, both Republicans and Democrats had been equally happy to apply this somewhat distorted version of democracy.

In New York, the link between politics and crime was (if anything) even more intimate and enduring. Tammany Hall, a by-word for political corruption and election-fixing, was heavily involved first with the Irish gangs of the nineteenth century and then with the Mafia in the twentieth. In 1949, Tommy "Three-Finger Brown" Lucchese made a handsome contribution to the re-election fund of Bill O'Dwyer. The contribution was in cash, in used bills of small denomination, and was paid when it would do the most good: two weeks *after* O'Dwyer's successful re-election.

ABOVE
William (Bill) O'Dwyer voting in 1939. Ten years later, shortly *after* his re-election as Mayor of New York City, O'Dwyer was to receive funds from Tommy Luchesse in small denomination, used bills.

ABOVE
William (Bill) O'Dwyer at his desk as Mayor of New York City. His receiving funds from known mobsters and his failure to prosecute Anastasia (see p62), among other things, led to suspicions of corruption.

LEFT
The Louisiana politician Huey P. ("the Kingfish") Long, who was notorious for his links with the mob, raises his arms as he speaks into the microphone.

In Louisiana, the links between Governor Huey "the Kingfish" Long and the Mob were equally lengendary, and in California in the 1940s the Mob were enthusiastic supporters of Richard Nixon. Of course, the Mob did not imagine that it could "buy" every politician it supported, but like any prudent businessman it supported whoever it thought would be best for its interests.

Big business used gangsters to break strikes and discourage unionization. A few broken bones on the picket line, or a stick of dynamite through the window of a union organizer, provided a quick and often efficient way of discouraging what the bosses saw as creeping socialism. To begin with the companies had hired their own "goons", but when there were ready-made private armies for hire, it was easier to sub-contract the work to them.

Union organizers used similar methods to defend their interests. Even honest union organizers found that they sometimes had need of pickets who were more at home with pickaxe handles and baseball bats than with lathes and contracts, and not all union organizers were honest. Organized crime was quick to spot the advantage of a "closed shop" in which workers were forced to pay their dues to the unions, while management could be terrorized into paying almost any rates the union cared to set, which provided a handsome cash-flow to be skimmed in the process.

BELOW
A large group of deputies about to attack a crowd of pickets in Pittsburgh, 1933. One man was killed and at least 15 injured in the violence that followed.

⊕
RIGHT
Mounted policemen move in to reinforce foot patrolmen who are trying to prevent pickets from the International Longshoremen's Association from entering a pier, 1954.

⊕
BELOW
Rioting strikers in Bayonne, New Jersey, 1915. This picture was taken just a few moments before one of the strikers was killed.

Combined with more traditional crime, whether strong-arm or "scam", politics, big business and the unions certainly created a cornucopia of criminal opportunity for the gangsters (as distinct from freelance petty criminals). It was into this fruitful arena that the first mafiosi arrived in New Orleans, as early as the 1880s (the *Times-Picayune* first drew attention to them in 1882). Over the next few years, they started a lucrative little protection racket on the waterfront, with members of rival gangs occasionally killing one another in an attempt to expand their turf: about 100 people were killed. Then, in late 1890, they made the serious error of killing the police chief, David Hennessy, who had threatened to expose "a criminal society, the Mafia". No fewer than 19 gangsters were indicted for conspiracy and murder, but justice was not served. Many witnesses and potential witnesses were intimidated or bribed, and perhaps unsurprisingly, all but three of the accused were acquitted. Even those three were not convicted because the jury could not reach a verdict.

Despite this, the solid citizens of New Orleans believed that the evidence against at least 11 of the mafiosi was conclusive, so in early 1891 they took the law into their own hands. Two suspects were

RIGHT
David Hennessy, the police chief of New Orleans, was assassinated in 1890 when he threatened to expose the Mafia.

BELOW
The New Orleans levees, shown in a woodcut from *Harper's Weekly*, 5 April 1884. The Mafia were running a waterfront protection racket in New Orleans as early as the 1880s.

strung up, seven were shot down in the jail yard by a "firing-squad" of local worthies, and two were shot repeatedly as they tried to hide in the kennel of the jailhouse guard dog.

BELOW
Canal Street, New Orleans, in the 1890s. Many Sicilian mafiosi arrived in New Orleans towards the end of the 19th century.

The consequences were considerable. Italy recalled its ambassador and severed relations with the United States, demanding compensation and punishment for the killers. Their ire was finally bought off with $25,000 paid to the dead men's relatives. The frightening part is that there are still Americans to this day who believe that lynch law is the answer to the Mafia: George Murray, in *The Legacy of Al Capone* (G. Putnam's Sons, New York, 1975), writes approvingly of this mob rule and of Brazilian death squads. Which is worse: the disease or the cure?

Nor was New Orleans the only place where Sicilians and other Italians were arriving. Driven out by the poverty of their homeland, they were also streaming into New York, which rapidly became the other main centre of Mafia activity. Only slowly did mafiosi begin to reach Chicago, where they would become almost synonymous with the city itself.

ANTONIO
SCAFFIDI

JOSEPH P
MACHECA

A.
BAGNETTO

JOHN
MATRANGA

PIETRO
MASTERO

THE MUSTACHE
PETES

In those early days, the Mafia was somewhat different from what it would later become. These were the times of the "Mustache Petes", so named for their heavy moustachios, who were normally at least as interested in *omertà* as in profit. They were the archetypal "Godfathers", the men who demanded (and got) "respect".

To this day, "respect" is one of the keys to understanding the behaviour of all gangsters. In the street slang of the early nineties, to "diss" someone is to be disrespectful to them; and "He dissin' me!" is all too likely to be the prelude to a murder. The person who does the "dissin'" must, however, be a small enough target to kill with relative impunity. The typical petty gang member knows all too well that if he hits "the Man", whether "the Man" in question is a policeman or is a senior gangster with another gang, his life is effectively forfeit. To kill someone who is "dissin'" you, however, when you know that there is a good chance you can get away with it, adds immensely to your self-esteem and to the status you have among your friends.

The moral code of the Mustache Petes, therefore, was not so different from the moral code of the Crips or the Bloods in a modern city. Honour was everything; profit was secondary. This explains why so many murders and robberies were (and are) committed over what appear to be trifling causes. The economic motive is often irrelevant.

In the United States of the late-nineteenth and early twentieth centuries, however, profit was becoming increasingly important; and if it was to be profit without honour, well, there were those

ABOVE
Five of the "Mustache Petes", from an illustration concerning the murder of Hennessey in an 1890 edition of *Harper's Weekly*.

who held their honour cheaply enough that this was not a problem. The "robber barons" of industry were getting *very* rich, *very* quickly. If the legitimate world was going that way, it was no great surprise that the underworld went that way too. The opportunities for both were available because of an incredible short-sightedness and hypocrisy, which has still not entirely disappeared from the United States.

The short-sightedness manifested itself in a desperate race for short-term gains, even if the long-term result would clearly be the destruction of natural resources and a workforce that was exploited almost to the point of civil war. Both, in the thinking of the robber barons, were infinite resources. The United States was simply too big to bankrupt – everyone could take what they wanted, legitimately or illegitimately, and there would still be more – while virtually unrestricted immigration meant an endless supply of new workers, customers and suckers. Nor is mention of civil war an exaggeration; company battles had attracted armed men at regimental strength by the era of the Wobblies (the Industrial Workers of the World), and the distraction of World War I was arguably all that stopped things from getting even worse.

After World War I Europe had torn itself to pieces, for the first time in the twentieth century, and a lot of the money that had been spent in the prosecution of the war had ended up in American pockets. American casualties were bad (approximately 125,000 killed), but Britain lost more than that on one *day* at the beginning of the battle of St. Quentin, 21 March, 1918, and total losses were about a million Britons. On both sides of the Atlantic, mere survival was grounds for celebration; and this is what American soldiers expected to come home to after the Armistice.

WANTED

information from **YOU** the taxpayer on the locations of

BOOTLEG STILLS

Moonshine stills in your locality like that pictured above, are robbing you of many thousands of dollars in Federal and State liquor taxes. Help your Government by reporting them, by mail or phone, to

ALCOHOL AND TOBACCO TAX DIVISION, INTERNAL REVENUE SERVICE

All communications held strictly confidential

Alcohol and Tobacco Tax
Post Office Box 224   Phone 9312
Bluefield, West Virginia

PURITANICAL
LEGISLATION

Unfortunately for them, and in the long run unfortunately for the whole United States, the 18th Amendment was passed on 16 January, 1919 to take effect one year later. Without the aid of organized crime, the party would have been somewhat flat.

The tide had been turning towards Prohibition for many years, not least with the Webb-Kenyon Act, passed (over presidential veto) in March 1913. That Act, which severely restricted interstate commerce in liquor, had already provided plenty of opportunities for liquor-running gangsters, and anyone with any political foresight could probably have guessed that things werer going to get *more* restrictive rather than less so.

Nor was Prohibition the only law on American statute books that looked frankly unworkable to a European. There were all sorts of others.

ABOVE RIGHT
A moonshine still in North Carolina. Although the equipment is crude, the demand for alcohol was such that people cared little for quality as long as they could get their hands on a drink.

LEFT
Even before the advent of Prohibition, bootleggers were in operation, avoiding heavy liquor taxes. Once Prohibition came, the "industry" of bootlegging expanded enormously, as did profits from the business.

RIGHT
Trucks being loaded with confiscated alcohol, 1923. Although the police had many successes in capturing illegal drink, the Mafia had far greater success in producing and distributing it.

ABOVE
Large amounts of illegal beer being poured into Lake Michigan in 1919. With Prohibition it seems that only the fish could get a legitimate drink!

One of the main ones was the puritanical prohibition of gambling. Some states permitted trackside betting at horse races, and others seem not to have been too worried either way; but the general legislative tenor was, as it has remained until recently, unbelievably anti-gambling.

For instance, slot machines are something which many Europeans do not even regard as gambling. In Europe, the "one-armed bandit" is as much an attraction for children as for adults. All

kinds of mechanical games of chance, generally for very low stakes, are available in all sorts of places. In the United States, by contrast, to this day the majority of bars do not have slot machines in them. In those states where there are slot machines, no one under the age of 18 or even 21 is allowed to play, and children are not even allowed within a yard or more of the machines. Controls on other forms of betting, such as lotteries, card tables and roulette wheels, are even more rigorous.

If people cannot easily gamble legally, they will generally find some way to gamble illegally. Once gambling is declared illegal, it makes it *much* easier for organized crime to run it. By definition, if it is illegal, then there are no legal controls; and if there are no legal controls, it is easier to run crooked games, to "skim" the profits (though that probably happens everywhere), and to encourage people to get in over their heads. However, as has already been mentioned, even where gambling is legal gambling debts are not legally enforceable, but are merely "debts of honour". The only way that the house can be sure of collecting credit is to send for the enforcers.

There is also a range of laws against prostitution: not just against living off immoral earnings, or against touting for business, but also against being a prostitute, visiting a prostitute, or transporting anyone across state lines for immoral purposes. That last one, incidentally, is not just concerned with white slavery; it can, in theory, be applied to an unmarried California couple who go to Las Vegas for a dirty weekend, or a couple of New Yorkers who go down to the Carolina beaches.

Given that no society has ever succeeded in rooting out prostitution, it is clear that any law against the oldest profession is at best a statement of society's disapproval. At worst, it is a hollow joke. To make everything associated with prostitution into a crime is sheer lunacy: the best that can be done is to try to protect girls from exploitation (even though they may volunteer for it), their customers from being robbed (even though they may deserve it), and all concerned from disease. The further underground you drive it, the better things are from the point of view of organized crime.

The setting of 18 as the age of consent is even more counter-productive. Labelling a normal human activity as a crime, and sending young men to prison for sleeping with young women, you create an automatic criminal class. For comparison with the United States, the age of consent in England is 16, and in France 15.

At this point, we begin to get into subjects that are more appropriate to the next chapter, which deals with the rise of organized crime during Prohibition. Before we do that, it is as well to take a quick look at how the Mafia is organized.

RIGHT
In the aftermath of a police raid on a gamblers' den in 1925, several van loads of bookmakers and gamblers were taken away from an address in East Street, New York.

ABOVE
Gambling takes place openly in a Nevada casino, 1910.

MAFIA RITUAL

First, and most importantly, it is essential to realize that *no one* can tell the whole story. Even if one of the great "Godfathers" were to tell all that he knew, it would not be the whole story. Initiation rituals (where they exist at all) have varied widely. The structure of the Mafia is shadowy enough that the terms we all *think* we know, like "Capo" and "Consigliere", may not even exist in many "families". The very word "Mafia" is by no means universally used: the Camorra and the Honoured Society merged with the Mafia, and some people (including the mobsters themselves) use two or more of these terms interchangeably. They may also refer to the Family, the Company, the Organization, "us", "people like us", "Good Fellows" and more. The term "Cosa Nostra" ("Our Thing") was popularized by the FBI when they finally realized that they could deny the existence of the Mafia no longer. Instead of admitting that he was wrong, J. Edgar Hoover said in effect, "There's no Mafia but there is a Cosa Nostra, and we have been keeping tabs on *them.*"

Having said all this, it is likely that some mafiosi did go through some sort of initiation ceremony with (at the least) a dagger, a revolver and a blood oath. Traditionally, the blood for the blood oath was drawn with a nick from a razor, though an even more symbolic pin-prick seems to have replaced that in later years. The oath itself was to

the effect that a member of the Mafia (or the Honoured Society, or the Camorra – all the reported ceremonies were much the same) lived by the dagger and the gun, so he should die by them if he broke the code of *omertà*. The code might or might not be spelled out, because most mafiosi would *know* what would happen to them if they were caught trifling with the affections of respectable (i.e. Mafia) girls, if they "squealed", or whatever.

In addition to the dagger, the revolver and the blood oath, there might be a Bible, a picture of the Blessed Virgin, or a rosary. It is not clear how Christian principles are reconciled to *omertà,* but many mafiosi describe themselves as devout Catholics. Some accounts tell of a picture of the candidate that is smeared with a bloody hand-print in his own blood; others describe a handshake, slippery with blood. The trouble is that a lot of these rituals may well be children of the fertile imagination of writers on the Mafia. Where they were actually used, it is not inconceivable that the Mafia borrowed them from invented accounts because they sounded like the sort of thing that desperadoes ought to do.

As for the requirement that any candidate should first prove his worthiness by killing someone, this seems to have been honoured more in the breach than the observance. Writers seem to love this idea, though, and glamorize it with the term "Making his Bones".

MAFIA
HIERARCHY

The "Made Men" (or "Button Men" or "Soldiers") who are admitted to the Mafia are chosen from the criminal hangers-on, who are constantly seeking admission to the Honourable Society. These hangers-on or associates may in many cases do the same sort of work as the Made Men: extortion, intimidation and even murder. They may handle money at a very low level, for instance as "runners" in a "numbers game". They may even act as "bagmen" who collect the loot from victims, though usually a Made Man or someone more senior will do this. They may handle straight hits, but for "buckwheat" jobs (torture killings to warn others), higher-ups may join in for the fun of it: Al Capone once beat three men to death with Indian clubs at a banquet given in their "honour", administering the *coup de grace* with a pistol.

The advantage of being a Made Man is that once you are in, *omertà* applies to you. You are much less likely to be casually disposed of, at least by your own people. You can claim the protection of your Family if you are insulted or harmed. This *may* apply to a mere associate, or it may not.

The next stage above Soldier or Made Man is *Caporegima* or Capo, the equivalent of a military officer; he is the liaison between the Soldier and the higher-ups. There will be a number of Capos in a Family. Next above the Capo comes the Underboss or right-hand man. The Underboss may be the successor apparent to the Boss, or he may be chosen because he complements the boss. A fruitful source of confusion here is that *Caporegima* is often translated as "lieutenant", while an Underboss is also referred to as the Boss's "lieutenant".

Somewhere between the Underboss and the Boss there is the *Consigliere* or "Adviser". This is *not* an official post; rather, it is a courtesy title accorded to a "Don" (any senior Mafia man, especially an old, experienced, *Sicilian* Mafia man). The job of the *Consigliere* is to advise the Boss and the Underboss, and to act as far as possible as a stabilizing influence. Because "as far as possible" is not very far, the importance of the *Consigliere* should not be overestimated.

BELOW
Mafia Boss Frank Costello, pictured in 1957, follows his lawyer (light coat) and is surrounded by his "Soldiers" and "Capos", together with hangers-on and journalists.

THE BOSS

Above them all, of course, is the Boss; and this is where life gets interesting. At any one time, there are a number of Families each with its own Boss. According to some, these Bosses are subordinate to a Commission, a gathering of Bosses, but this is not strictly accurate. A Commission or sit-down of Bosses has no power to bind any Boss except in so far as he consents to be bound. If he reckons he is stronger than the other Bosses and can afford to defy them, he will do so. Also, as some Families rise in importance others fall, and the right to sit on the Commission is not always established by a bloodless debate. This is why, although "organized crime" involves a good deal of co-operation between different Families, it should not be taken to mean that there is a seamless organization.

ABOVE
The most famous and perhaps the most publicly feared Boss of all time, Al Capone. Even in this carefully posed photograph, he looks a figure of considerable menace and power.

If there were, what need would there be for gangsters to kill one another – an activity to which they are demonstrably addicted?

One thing that there is *not* is a "Boss of Bosses" or "Supreme Godfather". This is an invention of the media and of the FBI, a familiar device for "demonizing" the adversary and explaining away one's own shortcomings. It is, after all, much easier to create an evil genius who is co-ordinating all crime, than it is to admit that both sides make mistakes, and that most of the time, the good guys make enough mistakes to leave the bad guys in business.

With the exception of the Boss, demotion is as possible as promotion; an Underboss can become a Capo, a Capo can become a Soldier. This is of course assuming that the demotion is not given with the assistance of a sawn-off shotgun.

THE FASCINATION OF EVIL

At the beginning of this chapter, I asked the semi-rhetorical question, "What is the Mafia?" Now, the time has come to ask another semi-rhetorical question: "What is the fascination of the Mafia?"

The answer, surely, is that in many ways we all want to *be* mafiosi: to command respect from other people; to be free of the workaday job, day in, day out; to be immune from the petty laws that we see springing up all around us; to have so much money that a $100 tip to a barman is of no consequence; to live an exciting life; to be able to snap our fingers and strike terror into the heart of some rude petty official or oaf; to have pretty girls hanging on our arms, and the knowledge that if we tire of them, we can immediately replace them with others equally beautiful, equally compliant. We are fascinated by evil.

When I say "we", I mean men; few women seem to crave the same things. There must be something, however, that attracts women to the Mob. *Omertà* has something for them, too – or at least, it has some things for some kinds of woman. There are jewels and furs for the bimbos. There is old-fashioned respect for the quiet wife. There is excitement, the edge of danger; there is the high of having sexual power over a killer. No doubt there have even been women behind the throne, though the masculine mythos of the Honoured Society does not record it.

The root of the fascination is that the lifestyle of the Mafia appears more glamorous and interesting than the lives that most of us lead.

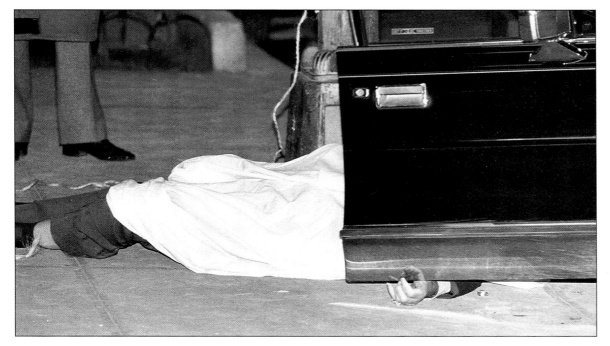

ABOVE
Joseph Lanza, the well-known mafioso, wearing handcuffs, is greeted by his wife, Ellen, in 1957. Women have no formal role in the Mafia, but nonetheless some seem drawn to the Mob.

LEFT
Two sides to the Mafia: the "glamorous" side is indicated by the open door of the luxurious limousine belonging to Mafia Boss Paul Castellano; the other side is indicated all too clearly by the body of Castellano lying under the door, gunned down in 1985.

UNHOLY ALLIANCE

Tʜᴇ ᴘᴀʀᴛɴᴇʀsʜɪᴘ ᴏꜰ "Lucky" Luciano and Meyer Lansky is a textbook example of organized crime in America. It shows that "The Mob" is far from exclusively Italian: Lansky was a Polish Jew. It shows that the men who *really* made the Mafia what it is today were not just ruthless killers, but also far-sighted businessmen. It shows that smart mobsters can live for a long time and die of natural causes: Luciano (1897–1962) died of a heart attack at 65, while Lansky (1902–1983) was over 80 when his heart gave out. It shows how straightforward, understandable business considerations caused the coalescence of the different gangs into a single Syndicate of organized crime, and how organized crime expanded geographically. It also shows that the Mafia is essentially an American organization. For during the lifetimes of Luciano and Meyer, the Mafia in Italy was crippled by *Il Duce* (Mussolini). Only an infusion of American techniques, assistance and even, surprisingly, government backing enabled it to survive.

Salvatore Lucania, who would change his name to Charles Luciano and become known as "Lucky" Luciano, was born in Sicily and came to New York in 1906 at the age of about nine. By the age of ten, he had been arrested for shoplifting and had already started a protection racket among younger schoolchildren: if they did not want to be beaten up on the way to school, it cost them money.

One of the few who stood up to him was a boy almost five years younger, Maier Suchowljansky. Meyer Lansky, as he was later known, not only resisted, but gave as good as he got. The two became firm friends.

By 1915–1916, Luciano who was not yet 20, had become a leading light of the Five Points Gang, who were the Italian successors to Irish gangs such as the Dead Rabbits and the Plug Uglies. The leader of the Five Points was known as Paul Kelly, though his given name was Paolo Antonini Vaccarelli. He used to take advantage of political and industrial demand for "muscle" as well as exploiting traditional avenues, such as murder for hire, extortion, numbers and protection rackets. A subsidiary of the Five Points Gang was the James Street Gang, run by Johnny Torrio. This was a "farm" or "youth" gang from which members might graduate to the Five Points Gang. By this time, though, both the Five Points Gang and the James Street Gang were on the way out, because labour reforms had removed their chief source of income. Luciano was looking for something new.

After 1920 he had found it: bootlegging. The previous few years had been devoted to general-purpose scams and mayhem, but with Meyer Lansky and Bugsy Siegel he had found a reliable new way to make money.

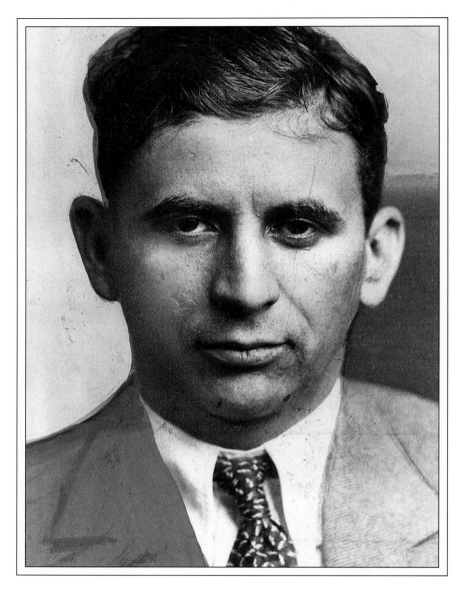

ABOVE
Meyer Lansky, born Maier Suchowljansky in 1902, a long-term friend and colleague of Lucky Luciano.

LEFT
Bugsy Siegal, pictured in 1930, was a determined killer who worked with Luciano and Lansky.

RIGHT
Lucky Luciano, born in 1897 in Sicily, was running a protection racket among fellow schoolchildren in New York by the age of ten.

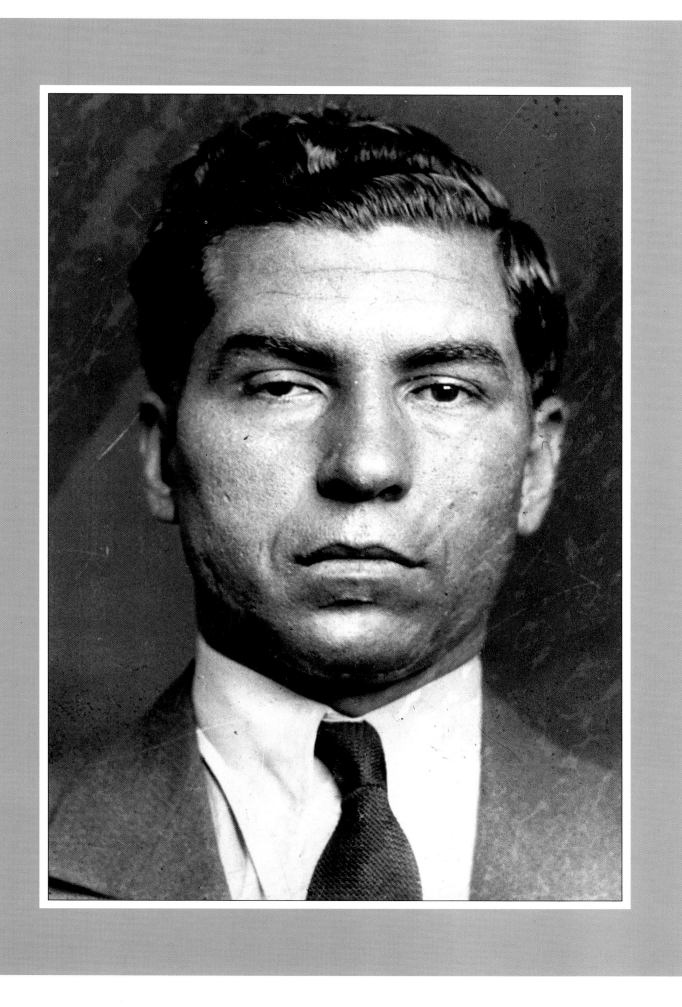

By this time, Lansky was 18 and Benjamin Siegel (1905–1947) was only 15, but the Bug and Meyer Mob was already a going concern. Bugsy was no genius, but he was a determined killer. The other mobsters called him a "cowboy", which was their term for a man who has to make a hit himself (or at least be present when the hit is made), rather than just leaving the contract to someone else. To his face, he was called "Ben" or "Mr. Siegel", but the nickname "Bugsy" came from the fact that he was a "bedbug" for killing: "crazy like a bedbug" was a standard description that was used of a psychotic mob killer.

It was in the 1920s that it became expedient for gangs to co-operate with each other more closely. After all, bootleg liquor had to come into the country (or be made inside the country), and then it had to be distributed to the countless speakeasies all around the country; and profits would clearly be higher all round if the different gangs did not waste too much money trying to cheat or fight one another. The stuff came in across the Canadian border; through major ports like New York and New Orleans, both of which had a heavy Mob presence on the waterfront; and through smaller ports where there had to be an infrastructure to receive and distribute it. This is why the focus of attention must shift temporarily away from New York.

CHICAGO

The biggest town on or near the Canadian border was Chicago. In 1919, the 20-year-old Alphonse "Al" Capone had moved to Chicago because of trouble with a couple of murder raps in New York

City. Big Jim Colisimo, Chicago's leading whoremaster, was the uncle of Johnny Torrio of James Street Gang notoriety, and Johnny was there to help him out. Torrio in turn found work for Capone to do.

Torrio was, by the standards of those around him, an old man. Born in 1882, he was already in his late thirties when Prohibition came. He had been involved in the narcotics trade since before World War I – so much for the old story that the Mafia abhorred drugs – and as early as 1909 he had started going to Chicago to help out Colosimo, an uncle by marriage. In 1915, Torrio moved full-time to the Windy City to work for and with his uncle, but he soon found that there were countless opportunities for extra crime that his uncle was just not interested in. Although to be fair, Colosimo was pushing 50 and had a very comfortable lifestyle, so he saw little need to exert himself greatly.

The (perhaps inevitable) result was that Big Jim was rubbed out by an imported New York hit man, Frankie Yale, on 11 May, 1920. Torrio and his protegé Capone were now free to make the city on the lake synonymous with organized crime.

Torrio seems to have been the first mafioso with a vision of a crime "Syndicate", where all the gangs collaborated as far as it was in their interest to do so. Within months of Big Jim's death, Torrio summoned all the Chicago gangs to a sit-down (Irish, Jewish, Polish, etc.), and gave them a simple choice: co-operation or war. Most chose co-operation, but a few chose war. The main holdouts were the (Italian) Gennas and the (Irish) O'Banions, and a three-sided gang war soon developed.

ABOVE
"Deannie" O'Banion, the leader of the O'Banions, was a psychopathic killer who was known as a gangster who lived by the "Gat". He is pictured here in 1924.

LEFT
The funeral of Charles Dion O'Banion in 1924. He was gunned down in his flower shop by three men from the Mafia.

THE O'BANIONS AND THE GENNAS

Charles Dion "Deanie" O'Banion, the leader of the O'Banions, personally killed anything from 25 men upwards (Chicago Chief of Police Morgan Collins was responsible for the estimate, but others credited him with 60 or more murders). He was a psychopath whose idea of a practical joke was packing the barrels of a shotgun with clay and then betting an acquaintance that he could not hit the side of a barn ten paces away. The gun would explode, with predictably unpleasant results.

He was also politically aware. When the Democrats paid best, he secured the Forty-Second and Forty-Third Wards for them, but when the the Republicans upped the ante, he made sure they got in. His biggest error was selling Johnny Torrio an illegal brewery for half a million dollars, just ahead of a police raid that he knew was coming: he told Torrio that he was going to take the money and quit the rackets. On 9 November, 1924, he was shot in his flower shop: one bullet in each cheek, two through the larynx, and two in the chest. It was a traditional Mafia hit, a firm handshake from one assassin as the other two shot him. The assassins were Frankie Yale (who had rubbed out Big Jim Colisimo), Albert Anselmi and John Scalise.

The O'Banion gang's Italian counterparts, the Gennas, reckoned they could survive because they had the police in their pockets. They even used to supply lists of other people's stills to the police, as any law-abiding citizen would. The first to go was "Bloody" Angelo Genna. He was trying to escape pursuers from the O'Banion gang when he crashed into a lamppost and was trapped behind the wheel, and could only watch as his executioner emptied a shotgun into him. Mike "the Devil" Genna was double-crossed by two of his own men, Albert Anselmi and John Scalise again, who had gone over to Johnny Torrio and Al Capone. They were taking him for a ride when the police ambushed them; they killed two policemen, wounded a third, and then left the mortally wounded Mike the Devil to be captured. Tony "the Gentleman" Genna was betrayed (again to Torrio's men) by Giuseppe "the Cavalier" Nerone, and the remaining Gennas – Pete, Sam and Jim – fled.

The O'Banions were still fighting, however, and on 24 January 1925 they ambushed Johnny Torrio. When he was down, they put four slugs into him, in the chest, arm and stomach. Incredibly, he lived, but he decided to retire. In February 1925, he took $30,000,000 as a retirement fund, and turned the whole business over to Al Capone. He was 43 years old, and he would not die until April 1957, when he was 75 years old. He was sitting in a barber's chair, Chicago-style with his face to the door so he could see who walked in, and he had a heart attack. Shortly afterwards he died in bed.

ABOVE
The funeral of "Bloody" Angelo Genna, who was killed with a shotgun by a member of the O'Banion gang after a car chase.

THE CAPONE ERA

"Scarface" Capone was now 26 years old, and he found himself running an organized crime syndicate with over a thousand people on the payroll and outgoings of $300,000 a week; the equivalent of better than $3,000,000 at today's rates. Unlike Torrio, Capone was no intellectual, but he was bright enough and he was lucky. In 1926, for example, the remnants of the O'Banion gang put a thousand rounds into his headquarters at the Hawthorne Hotel, mostly from Thompson guns. An entire motorcade drove slowly past the hotel, shooting as they went. Astonishingly, hardly anyone was hurt.

Where did the money come from? From all over, but principally from three sources which were not even illegal in large parts of the world: booze, betting and broads.

The booze was the real money-spinner. Any novel of the 1920s shows that booze was as much a part of everyday life then as it is now. It was much rougher booze, usually distilled only once without much attention to "tailings" (the poisonous alcohols at either end of the distillation run) and sold fresh. "Bathtub" gin could be made from potatoes and raisins and sugar, "grappa" from grapes and sugar, and "moonshine" from corn. Those who wanted something better were often sold Canadian, Scotch or Irish whiskey, which had been "cut" with the cheap stuff in the proportion of anything from ten per cent to 90 per cent. Some "hootch" was literally lethal, if drunk in sufficient quantities, and blindness was a serious risk for the over-enthusiastic imbiber. Despite these drawbacks, bootlegging was not even regarded as a crime by most people.

Betting was viewed in much the same way, since many – perhaps most – people like to bet. The man who makes this possible is a public servant, not a public enemy. It was true that some people got in over their heads, and had their legs broken when they did not pay, but the vast majority of gamblers were totally happy with the way the system worked.

And the broads? Well, it was a less self-analytical age. Prostitution was ritually deplored, of course: the term "Fallen Woman" was still

commonplace, although the men who visited whores did not worry too much about it. Catching a disease was their main concern, not the ultimate fate of the hooker who serviced them. Most of the girls looked as if they were having a good time (especially if you wanted to believe that they were, as most of their patrons inevitably did), so the general attitude was that it was technically illegal, but who cared?

Therefore, with three "victimless" crimes and a booming economy, it was no wonder that money meant nothing to a mobster like Capone. There was just too much of it being pressed into his hands. Even a legitimate businessman who owns distilleries, breweries and casinos is likely to be a

BELOW
Al Capone had this armour plated Cadillac made especially for him by General Motors. Such a vehicle was a wise precaution for a mobster in the Chicago of the 1920s and 1930s, if he could afford such a luxury.

LEFT
Al Capone smiles with confidence, although he was on his way to the Federal Penitentiary in Atlanta when this picture was taken.

millionaire, and when you have Thompson guns to take care of awkward business rivals, it gives a whole new meaning to "levelling the playing field".

A Tommy gun cost $175, and it was a perfectly legal weapon that could be mail-ordered, at least for the first few years after its commercial introduction in 1920. It was a beautifully made weapon, which inspired a tremendous pride of ownership, and the fact that it sprayed its big, heavy .45 calibre bullets around very slowly and noisily was an advantage rather than a drawback. Its very little kick (the cartridge is only a pistol cartridge, and the gun is very heavy) meant that the "Chicago Typewriter" was a pleasure to fire. "The gun that made the Twenties roar" is surely another part of the enduring and particular fascination of the Mafia.

ST VALENTINE'S DAY

The Tommy gun was the star of the St Valentine's Day Massacre, when the leaders of "Bugs" Moran's remnants of the O'Banion gang were mown down with sub-machine-gun fire. George "Bugs" Moran escaped. He saw Capone's men dressed as police officers and (like his henchmen) assumed it was a police shakedown, and decided to stay out of the way until it was over. He was lucky he did.

A few days after the Massacre, Al Capone personally beat three men to death with a gift-wrapped Indian club: Hop Toad Giunta, John Scalise and Albert Anselmi. They had been conspiring to turn against him and kill him (Anselmi and Scalise had already switched allegiance from the Gennas), so he invited them to a dinner in their honour, and killed them by way of after-dinner entertainment.

Although the Massacre was effective in establishing Capone's final control, public outrage was so great that, for once, Capone and the other bootleggers were not seen as public heroes. At a big "sit-down" in Atlantic City, Scarface was severely criticized and was advised to go to jail for a while to take the heat off the Mob. He obligingly did this, going down for a short spell on a (carefully orchestrated) gun charge in Philadelphia.

The public drew the obvious (but wrong) conclusion that if Capone was unable to escape even a minor rap like that, he would certainly be unable to get away with mass murder.

As it turned out, Capone's sun was setting, just as it appeared to be at its brightest. He was caught on what has since become almost a traditional charge for top mobsters, income tax evasion, and sent down for 11 years in 1931. He was incarcerated first in the federal prison at Atlanta, and then (after 1934) on Alcatraz. The pressures of "the Rock" were notorious for driving prisoners "stir crazy" even without untreated tertiary syphilis, from which Al was suffering. By the time he was released in 1939, he was only occasionally lucid. He lived on for another eight years in Florida, finally dying on 25 January 1947, 32 years and one day after the Johnny Torrio ambush.

THE FUTURE
TAKES SHAPE

Although it was Chicago that caught the world's imagination in the 1920s and 1930s, it was back in New York that the future of organized crime was being hammered out.

"Lucky" Luciano was a Sicilian, but (like Capone) he was an equal-opportunity villain. Ignoring advice to stay away from Frank Costello, described by fellow Sicilians as a "dirty Calabrian", he fell in with all the big names in New York in the early 1920s, among whose leaders were two Jews, Arnold Rothstein and Dutch Schultz.

Arnold Rothstein is still remembered by collectors of baseball trivia as the man who "fixed" the 1919 World Series. "Fixing" was his speciality. Born in 1882, he was just entering his fifth decade as the Roaring Twenties got under way, and he was a *very* smart individual. Any gang leader with an IQ above room temperature went out of his way to seek Rothstein's advice, and anyone who had problems with a bootlegging case was well advised to have Rothstein spread the "grease" around. Of

the 6,902 cases in the Rothstein era, 400 never came to trial and 6,074 were dismissed in court. His own profits from Prohibition came from importing the good stuff, which lent a thin veneer of drinkability to the better variety of hootch; he was, therefore, much in demand among *all* bootleggers. He died violently, it is true, but there are two schools of thought about who rubbed him out on 4 November, 1928 at the Park Central Hotel. One school maintains that he was taken out by (or at the behest of) two disaffected gamblers to whom he had lost $320,000 in a marathon, non-stop poker match that lasted from 8 September to 10 September. Certainly, Nigger Nate Raymond and Titanic Thompson had grounds to resent him, in that he welched on his debts, complaining that the game had been fixed. The alternative theory states that Dutch Schultz had him killed in order to expand his own empire. Given that the Mob could probably have caught and killed a couple of Californian outsiders, the second theory has its attractions.

Dutch Schultz was much more the mobster of popular imagination. Unlike Luciano and

BELOW
A group of officials inspect a large drugs cache, the one-time property of Arnold Rothstein. Although Rothstein was an intellectual as mobsters go, he still had to make a living along traditional lines.

ABOVE
Arthur Flegenheimer, a.k.a. Dutch Schultz, in the consulting room of the New York courthouse where he faced charges of tax evasion – like many gangsters before and after him – in 1935.

Rothstein, he did not believe in negotiations, "sit-downs", or deals. He believed in the gun. His fortune came from the numbers racket, which he came to dominate by the simple expedient of terrorizing (and frequently killing) the small-time black operators who actually ran the illegal lotteries. Once he dominated it, he vastly increased his take as a result of mathematical manipulations by Otto "Abbadabba" Berman. Berman's theorems

enabled him to keep the payout to a minimum, while maintaining the illusion (or possibly even the actuality) of fairness. Although Schultz kept his other Capos on a tight financial rein, Berman was paid $10,000 a week. As a matter of interest, Arthur Flegenheimer (Dutch Schultz's real name) is said to have chosen his alias so that it would fit on the length of a newspaper headline: he loved to read about himself.

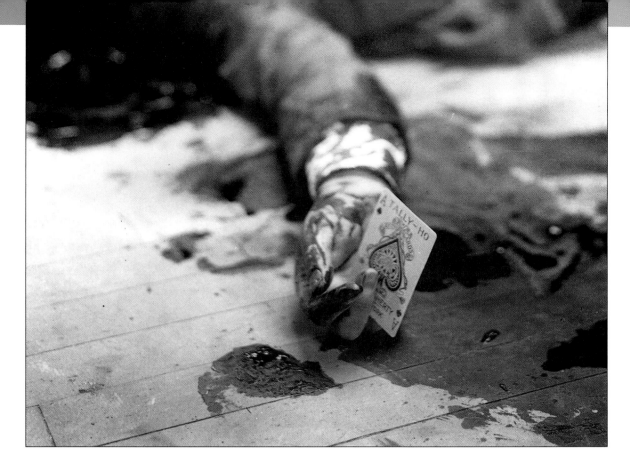

RIGHT
The body of Giuseppe Massaria, gunned down while he was playing pinochle in a Coney Island restaurant, 1931.

THE
TRIUMVIRATE

Between them Luciano, Rothstein and Schultz seem to have agreed that the "Mustache Petes" were the big barrier to making serious money. Rather than trying to work together, the old Sicilian dons were fighting battles that had their roots in the Old Country. These blood feuds, and straightforward peasant suspicion of "outsiders", stopped them from creating a "syndicate".

At the time, Giuseppe Massaria ("Joe the Boss") headed the largest Mafia Family in New York, and he was a classic "Mustache Pete". Luciano was his Underboss, and Luciano had eyes on promotion. During the Castellammarese Wars of 1928–1931, Joe the Boss was fighting Salvatore Maranzano, another "Mustache Pete", and almost all of the younger Mob men on both sides were heartily sick of the fighting. They were waiting for one Boss to kill the other, so that they could stop the war and go back to making money.

Eventually, in 1931, Luciano bumped off Massaria, using three of his own men and Bugsy Siegel. Maranzano then committed a fatal mistake and made Luciano his own Underboss.

Maranzano's problem seems to have been that he was blinkered by the hierarchical structure of the old Mafia, and he envisioned his own position as being the "Boss of Bosses" (*Capo di Tutti Capi*). What he did not realize was that the age of the Robber Baron was all but over; the day of the Corporate Pirate was dawning. He thought he could take out Capone and Luciano, his chief rivals, but Capone went to prison and Luciano took out Maranzano on 10 September, 1941.

Maranzano's death marked the end of the old Mafia in the United States. Henceforth, it would be run more with an eye to profit, and less with an eye to Sicilian village feuds. What was more, the New York Mafia would now become what the Chicago Mafia had been for a decade, a multi-ethnic crime syndicate.

There is a persistent legend that immediately after Maranzano's assassination, Luciano also slaughtered a large number of other "Mustache Petes" in "The Night of the Sicilian Vespers", a title that recalls the original foundation of the Mafia. There is no evidence for this in the crime records of the period. Many old-time mafiosi had already died, either of natural causes or of massive lead poisoning. If there were any left to yearn for the old days, they had the sense to do their yearning out of range of Lucky Luciano.

A few months before he died, Maranzano, the self-styled *Capo di Tutti Capi*, had, however, laid the foundations and mapped the structure for the empire that Luciano was to inherit. At a huge "sit-down" of about 500 gangsters, he proposed that the New York Mafia should be divided into five Families; that each should consist of a Boss, and Underboss, *Capos* and "Soldiers"; and that he, Maranzano, should head the lot. He is also credited with the invention of the term "Cosa Nostra", though it may simply be that he proposed formalizing a term that was already in use.

Although Maranzano never lived to see his ideas come to fruit, he can be credited (jointly with Luciano) with turning the Mafia into a distinctly American organization. In the Old Country times were hard and the Mafia was increasingly on the defensive.

LEFT
Giuseppe Massaria ("Joe the Boss") at one time headed the largest Mafia family in New York. He was killed by the henchmen of Lucky Luciano in 1931, the year of this photograph.

MUSSOLINI

AND THE

MAFIA

In 1922, a gangster of an entirely different kidney had come to power in Italy – Benito *Il Duce* Mussolini. Despite his many shortcomings, Mussolini did have at least two good points. The one that is best known is that he made the trains run on time, something that no Italian government has seriously attempted before or since, and the other is that he was *extremely* anti-Mafia.

This was mainly a matter of political expediency. Italy was barely in control of Sicily, and Mussolini wanted to remove the old, lazy, corrupt local officials and replace them with his own men. The Mafia, however, *liked* having lazy and corrupt local officials, because it made their life much easier. When *Il Duce* visited Sicily in 1924, he was publicly humiliated by Don Ciccio Cuccia, the mayor of Piana dei Greci and also a local Mafia Boss. Don Ciccio made it clear that it was his men, and not Mussolini's fascist bodyguards, who guaranteed his safety. He also made sure that the audience at one public speech consisted only of "twenty village idiots, one-legged beggars, bootblacks and lottery-ticket sellers".

Mussolini's police were not too fussy about rules of evidence or other legal niceties. Instead they fought the Mafia on their own terms, by terror and suspicion. They may have been the first to use electric shocks to the genitals as a means of torture, and another favoured technique was to insert a funnel in a suspect's mouth and force him to swallow salt water until his stomach was drum-tight. They had little difficulty in extracting

confessions, even if the accused party was not strictly guilty. Hundreds of innocent people were convicted, along with hundreds more who were far from innocent. Many mafiosi gave up their criminal activities, a good number died, and somewhere between 500 and 1000 of them escaped on the "Mussolini Shuttle" to the United States. Their escapes were masterminded by Don Vito Cascio Ferro, already in his sixties, and the one man that even Maranzano regarded as a legitimate *Capo di Tutti Capi.*

Don Vito was no stranger to the United States. He fled to New York in about 1899 or 1900, when the Sicilian police were pressing him a little too closely about a kidnapped baroness, and stayed for several years, although he had to move rather smartly to New Orleans as the result of police interest in another murder. By 1909, he was back in Sicily and is widely believed to have been responsible for the death of New York police detective Joseph Petrosino, who was on the island in that year gathering evidence about deporting mafiosi. Don Vito was the classic "Mustache Pete": tall, lean, aristocratic-looking, frock-coated with a pleated skirt, flowered cravat and wide-brimmed fedora. He also seems to have been inept at avoiding the attentions of the police. Although when he was finally arrested by Mussolini's police they were unable to make any legitimate charges stick, and were reduced to framing him. He died in prison in 1932, aged about 72.

The Mafia was declining in importance in its home country just as its power and wealth were increasing in the New World. Of course, the Sicilian Mafia had never had a fraction of the wealth (or the opportunity for making it) that existed in the United States.

ABOVE
The dictator Benito Mussolini was an arch enemy of the Mafia in Italy. His actions were one reason why a number of Italian mafiosi moved to the United States during the 1920s and 1930s.

THE
COMMISSION

Although "Lucky" Luciano could have claimed the title of "Boss of Bosses", he realized that to do so would probably result in a drastically reduced life expectation. Instead, he set up the "commission", along with Joe Adonis (actually Joe Doto, an Italian born in 1902); Dutch Schultz; Louis Lepke (Louis Buchalter, another Jew with extensive trade union contacts); Frank Costello; and his old friend and colleague Meyer Lansky.

Between them, this panel probably comprised the greatest collection of criminal talent ever assembled in one place. In short order, they controlled (alphabetically) all significant bootlegging; gambling; labour rackets; loan-sharking; narcotics trafficking; and prostitution.

Most of these are fairly self-explanatory, but "labour rackets" may require a little explanation.

RIGHT
Meyer Lansky was one of the "commission" set up by Lucky Luciano. Lansky is shown here descending the steps of a New York court in 1958.

BELOW
Dutch Schultz, one of Lucky Luciano's "commission", photographed in front of the New York Federal Court Building in 1935.

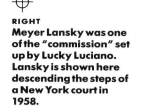

THE LABOUR
RACKETS

The days when management and organized labour each hired goons from the Mob to slug it out were all but gone (though they still survived on a modest scale; as recently as the mid-1980s, Frank Purdue of chicken-raising fame admitted seeking help from the Mob to oppose unionization at his factories), and the Circulation Wars when rival newspaper barons had hired thugs to destroy news-stands carrying rivals' papers were gone, too. There were however plenty of opportunities for a resourceful thug to make money in other ways.

One way was (and is) simple extortion, which is particularly effective in the fashion trade and the restaurant business. In both of these, the cost of the raw materials is comparatively low when compared with the cost of the finished product. Another modest overhead will hardly be noticed by the customer, or so goes the Mob's argument. In the 1980s, the "parsley racket" was apparently popular. Restaurants had to buy Mob parsley, at ten times the market price.

Another possibility is "sweetheart" union deals, in which the Mob keeps unionized employees in line. The employer pays for a stable labour force and the employees just pay.

Yet another is control of transport. For example, he who controls the transport of bread controls its freshness and when it arrives in the shops. If you want your bread to arrive fresh and on time, you

ABOVE
A press conference held by Thomas E. Dewey as Special Prosecutor at his New York offices in 1937. He had just successfully prosecuted men involved in restaurant union racketeering.

might need to pay a penny a loaf to make sure things turn out that way. Or again, if you want your garbage hauled away, you had better pay the men who do it, and the men who allow them to do it. At this point, given the endemic waste and self-interest in the average City Hall, the line between taxes and extortion begins to look very fine indeed. You may also find that if you do not pay off the right people, you receive unwelcome visits from official inspectors who are either in the pay of the Mob or who are tipped off.

The docks (and today, the airports) are another fruitful field. If you want your stuff to arrive *at all,* instead of being siphoned off while it is being unloaded, it will cost you. Also, if you are a criminal looking for something to steal, it helps to know what is coming in, what is "protected" and what is not, and who can be relied upon to look the other way as you leave with it.

The list goes on. A corrupt union boss is especially useful. He lends the Mob money for "high-risk" investments (like casinos, which are no risk at all in the right hands) and launders other money via its pension fund. The "working stiffs"? Who cares about them? Certainly not the union boss, who may be getting several times his legitimate salary from the Mob. If a union will not play, the Mob put in their own non-union labour, pays them well under union rates, charges more than union rates, and pockets the difference. At worst, the union leader may be bribed to keep his men out, so that the Mob can put theirs in.

THE REMOVAL OF
DUTCH SCHULTZ

By 1935, Dutch Schultz had become an embarrassment. His "Whack 'em" style of management did not find favour with the other Bosses, and matters came to a head when Schultz wanted to hit Thomas E. Dewey, the New York District Attorney and special prosecutor who was hurting him in the pocket book. The request was unanimously turned down, for the simple, practical reason that killing a federal prosecutor would bring too much heat. Schultz, however, had apparently devised a plan and had even staked out the killing ground. On 23 October, 1935, he was shot by unknown assailants (though it is generally believed that they were acting under Luciano's orders), and died a couple of days later.

Ironically, it was Dewey who sent Luciano down in 1936 on a charge of compulsory

BELOW
New York District Attorney Thomas E. Dewey – later to be Governor Dewey – whose successes against the mob led Dutch Schultz to want him assassinated.

prostitution ("white slaving"). It is by no means clear that Luciano was actually guilty of the precise crime with which he was charged, but it earned him a sentence of 30 to 50 years, the longest ever handed down for such an offence. It was widely believed in the underworld that his conviction was based on the word of people who were lying to keep themselves out of jail.

Luciano was not to be deterred by so minor a detail as being behind bars. From 1936 to 1946 he ran the Syndicate from prison. Then, in an amazing twist, Governor Dewey (as he now was) freed Luciano on parole. In fact, World War II was a time of mixed fortunes for the Mafia Bosses; but this is the subject of the next chapter, along with "Murder, Incorporated".

MURDER, INC.

WHEN LUCKY LUCIANO bumped off Salvatore Maranzano, but still put Maranzano's dream of a syndicate into action, it was clear that there was going to have to be an enforcement arm of some kind. Petty enforcement such as beatings and broken arms could easily be taken care of by regular "Soldiers", or by their higher-ups if they enjoyed it, but the trouble with murders was that the law enforcement agencies tended to take a dim view of them.

The answer was to create a murder machine, which would make killings all but impossible to trace. Surprisingly, this is not particularly difficult.

MURDER
INVESTIGATIONS

Consider how a murder investigation works. First, you need a motive. The vast majority of murders that are cleared up are solved because the pool of suspects is relatively small. The painstaking gathering of evidence and the skilled questioning of the right people, will determine which of four or five suspects committed the murder. Often, it is merely a question of proving that one person, the only believable candidate, did it.

Also, because murder is mostly a domestic affair, there is a good chance that someone, somewhere in the accused's circle of friends, will be able to put up a good alibi or (more likely) to supply the clues that put the killer away. If the murderer is known to the victim, as is almost invariably the case in "domestic" murders, the chances are that he is also known to at least some of the victim's friends.

Finally, because murder is such an awful crime, the majority of those who knew the deceased are going to want the murderer put away. Even those who did not know the deceased have an interest in clearing up the crime: they fear that they or their loved ones could be next.

None of these circumstances occurs in a properly organized gangland killing. The motive certainly exists, but it is likely to be a very diffuse motive, which it is almost impossible to explain conclusively. The pool of people who might want someone dead is very large, so getting any kind of lead is correspondingly difficult.

Then, if the murderer is a stranger to the victim, he is probably a stranger to the victim's friends and associates as well. This is why the term "out-of-town hit man" is so commonly

BELOW
Another victim of a Mafia hit, but what was the real motive for the killing? The man who pulled the trigger was probably only motivated by the pay-off from his masters.

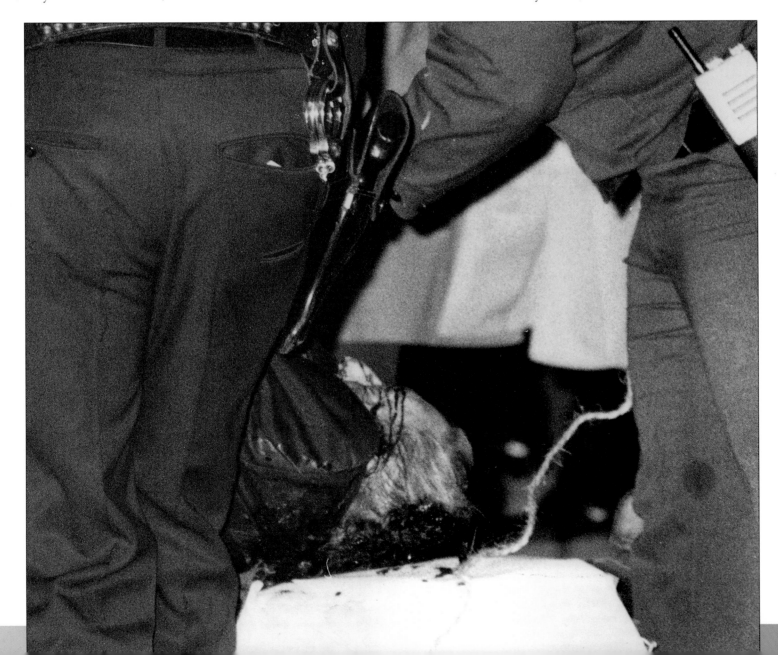

encountered. No one, not even the victim, recognises him or has any idea of his movements.

There is also very little incentive for anyone to clear up the murder. If the victim was a known villain, as is normally the case in a gangland killing, the unofficial police reaction may well be satisfaction. They will go through the motions of a murder investigation, but they may not always be too worried about finding out who did it. There is certainly no incentive for other villains to turn anyone in, because they know that there is a good chance that they will also end up dead, and they

BELOW
Albert Anastasia, perhaps the best known member of the Murder, Inc., team and believed by some to have been the real head of the organization.

also know that their livelihood ultimately depends on this sort of "enforcement". Equally, although outsiders may have less to fear from the Mob than they think, there is always the feeling that it is as well to keep as quiet as possible, just in case there are any unpleasant consequences. This is all the more true when witnesses or others in a position to give valuable information can rationalize, "Well, the world is better off without that guy anyway".

This was the premise on which Murder, Incorporated was founded; and it added a few wise twists of its own.

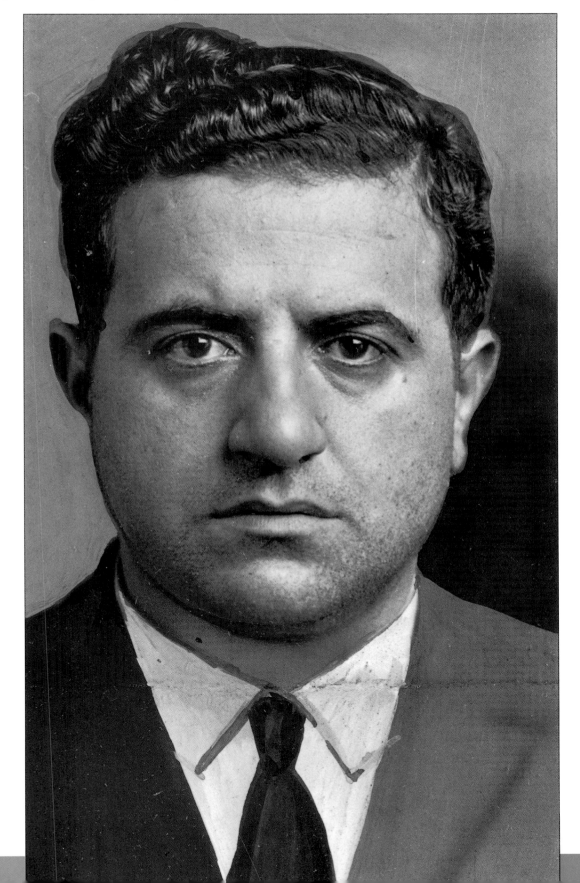

THE CODE OF
PRACTICE

First, Murder, Inc. killed only mobsters. Killing "civilians", police, politicians or reporters was bad for business: it brought too much heat. As Bugsy Siegel said, both philosophically and prophetically, "We only kill each other".

Second, Murder, Inc. killed mobsters only for good business reasons. Personal vendettas, including affairs of the heart, were no business of the Syndicate. Likewise, political killings (whether of other gangsters or of outside figures) were interdicted. The main reasons for a "hit" were bad business dealings, or clear and present danger to the Mob. Such clear and present danger might come from an informer, or from a "bedbug" who took excessive risks. Usually, too, the hits were clean, "in and out" jobs; "buckwheat" or torture killings were too risky. There were plenty of other gangland murders, for personal or political reasons, but they were not carried out by Murder, Inc.

Third, Murder Inc. took very good care that it should be very hard indeed to trace who had given the actual orders for a hit. The hit man might be picked up, but in the unlikely event that he wanted to "sing", he could only identify the Capo or possibly only the fellow Soldier who had given him the instructions. The investigating team would then have to interrogate that person to see who had given him the orders. If they could all they would have would be hearsay evidence, which is not admissible in a court of law (though inadmissible evidence does get used from time to time, and once an attorney has said it in court, no jury is ever going to discount it entirely). At each stage, the investigators have to contend with *omertà,* and with plain fear of what might happen if the person under interrogation gives the name of someone too high up the tree.

RIGHT AND TOP RIGHT
Police pictures of Joe Adonis, taken in 1937. Adonis was a key figure in Murder, Inc., largely because of his ability to keep a cool head.

THE MANAGEMENT AND THE HIT MEN

To this day, it is not totally clear who set up Murder, Inc. The name itself, "Murder, Inc.", was a media invention. There seems to have been no particular name for the enforcement arm of the Mafia inside the Honoured Society itself. It seems likely, though, that Murder, Inc. was both a creation of the existing Syndicate and the cement of a newer, larger one. For instance, Moe Dalitz of Cleveland is widely believed to have been intimately involved with the setting up of the organization, and its decade or so of success may be attributed to his cool head.

A man who believed in negotiation and compromise whenever possible, Moe nevertheless accepted that in the last resort, violence was the answer. Because he preferred to use violence as rarely as possible, he had great respect for it; and because he used it coldly, rationally and (relatively) sparingly, he was renowned for using it effectively. The advice of such a man was obviously extremely valuable when setting up anything as potentially risky as Murder, Inc.

The actual day-to-day administration of Murder, Inc. was entrusted to Louis Lepke, though the members of the Commission or Syndicate always had the power of veto. Murder, Inc. probably killed between 400 and 500 people in the

ABOVE AND LEFT
Louis Lepke (Buchalter), after a career of racketeering, took over the day-to-day running of Murder, Inc.

10 or 12 years it was in existence, and every single hit was made with the approval (tacit or explicit) of the big guys such as Lucky Luciano, Meyer Lansky and Frank Costello.

Louis Lepke was born in 1897; "Lepke" is an abbreviation of "Lepkeleh" or "Little Louis" in Yiddish, and was apparently the name that his mother Mrs. Buchalter used for her wayward son. In the 1920s, he and "Gurrah" Shapiro ("Gurrah here" was how he pronounced "Get out of here", one of his favourite phrases) had worked for Little Augie Orgen in the all-American business of strike-breaking, so he was no stranger to violence. Indeed, Lepke's first promotion came when he and Shapiro ambushed and killed Little Augie in 1927, in order to take over the business for themselves.

Lepke's chosen assistants for Murder, Inc. were his old sidekick Gurrah Shapiro and Albert Anastasia, though Joe Adonis also worked with the team from time to time.

Anastasia is of course the best-known member of the team, and indeed many people believe that he and not Lepke was the head. There are various reasons for this, but one of the strongest is that the "Soldiers" were mostly Sicilian mafiosi who could not get rid of the idea that only Sicilians could be in command. They believed that people like Lansky and Lepke might be advisers, but that they could not vote because they were not Sicilian or even Italian. As it happened, this pretence suited the Jewish mobsters very well, because it enabled them to distance themselves from the public opprobrium that sometimes attached to the Mob. In truth, race or religion was (and remains) a secondary consideration in organized crime. One of the least likely of gangsters was Murray "the Camel" Humphreys, a Welshman, who may have received his nickname either from his fondness for camel-hair coats or as an obvious play on his last name.

Albert Anastasia was born in Italy in 1903 and jumped ship in Brooklyn as a teenager sometime between 1917 and 1920, He rapidly became a man of importance in the Longshoremen's Union, not least because of his willingness to kill at the drop of a hat. In his early twenties, he was actually on Death Row in Sing Sing for 18 months as a result of killing another longshoreman, but four critical witnesses failed to turn up for his retrial – or for anything else, ever again – so he went free. This was to be the pattern of any subsequent trials: anyone foolish enough to let it be known that he might possibly testify against Anastasia usually ended up dead. This, rather than innocence, is how he managed to die in a barber's chair instead of the electric chair – he

RIGHT
The body of Albert Anastasia lies near the barber's chair in which he was murdered.

BELOW RIGHT
Joe Adonis in his cabin as he travels by ship to Italy, having chosen exile over prison.

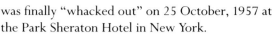

BELOW
Murray "the Camel" Humphreys, a one-time associate of Al Capone, was a seemingly unlikely mobster.

was finally "whacked out" on 25 October, 1957 at the Park Sheraton Hotel in New York.

Joe Adonis, born Joe Doto in Montemarano in 1902, was essentially a small-time punk who was promoted beyond his abilities as a result of loyalty to cleverer men who needed reliable, cool-headed muscle. His main function in Murder, Inc. appears to have been to restrain Anastasia, who might otherwise have been even more kill-crazy than he was. Like Anastasia, he avoided prison for a long

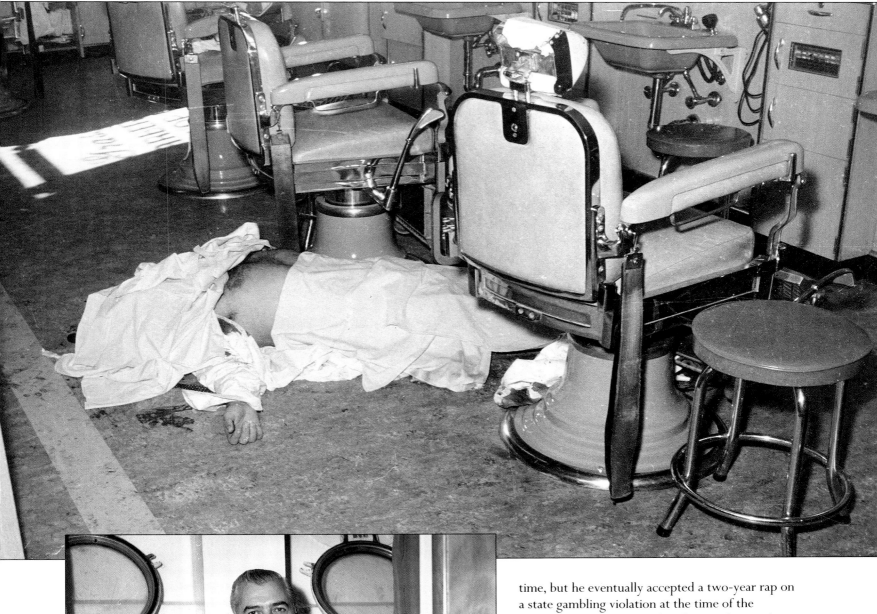

time, but he eventually accepted a two-year rap on a state gambling violation at the time of the Kefauver hearings. After that, he was deported and ended his days in comfort in Milan.

Under these luminaries were several wonderfully named hit men, such Vito "Chicken Head" Gurino, Blue Jaw Magoon, Abe "Kid Twist" Reles and Frank "the Dasher" Abbandando, as well as Pittsburg Phil Strauss and Happy Maione. All were professionals, and some of the stories behind the nicknames are interesting. "Chicken Head" used to shoot the heads off chickens by way of target practice; Happy Maione had a permanent scowl; and "the Dasher" apparently acquired his nickname when he was hired to hit a longshoreman early in his career, but became the pursued rather than the pursuer when his gun misfired. He then ran around the block so fast that he caught up with his victim from behind, and put three bullets into him. All of these, and others, used to hang out at Midnight Rose's, a 24-hour drug store in Brooklyn at the corner of Saratoga and Livonia.

"KID TWIST"
RELES SINGS

It was "Kid Twist" Reles, whose nickname came from the way he habitually chewed candy canes, who was to prove the downfall of Murder, Inc. About three years after Dutch Schultz had been taken out, as described in the last chapter, Reles was pulled in on suspicion of homicide.

Worried for his own safety, in case someone else incriminated him, Reles began to "sing" on the grand scale. He was promised that he would not be prosecuted for any murder in which he had participated if he told the police everything about it. He took his cue from Kipling's "six honest serving men": he told them what, why, when, how, where and who. In a matter of weeks, he had enabled the police to clear up no fewer than 49 murders in Brooklyn alone.

Over the course of more than a year, Reles helped to put together a case against Louis Lepke himself, as well as against Louise Capone (no

BELOW
Abe "Kid Twist" Reles.

RIGHT
Lepke on trial after information from Reles.

BELOW RIGHT
Reles "sings" to U.S. Attorney Palmer.

relation) and Mendy Weiss, two of Lepke's sidekicks. Understandably, he was never left alone, not even when he was sleeping, but on the night of 12 November, 1941 his body was found about 20 feet from the foot of the building in which he had been staying on the sixth floor under the protection of six of New York's finest. It was of course a suicide, though years later Meyer Lansky and Doc Stacher would reveal that $100,000 had been spread around to facilitate this act of self-destruction.

The Syndicate apparently made no serious attempt to rescue those of its own who were already marked for the chair, but if Reles had been allowed to "sing" any more, a number of other Mob high-ups might have found themselves in similarly embarrassing positions. After all, Reles was high enough up in the organization to point the finger at a lot of people. There were, however, two very interesting riders to his death.

THE FALL OF
MURDER, INC.

One concerned the case against Anastasia himself. William O'Dwyer, then the Brooklyn district attorney and later the Mayor of New York, maintained that the "perfect case" against Anastasia had gone out of the window along with Reles. When Anastasia was arraigned before a grand jury in 1945, O'Dwyer's failure to prosecute was castigated by the jury as negligent, incompetent and flagrantly irresponsible, with the rider that it was also "revolting". Their implication, a view widely shared by the press, was that O'Dwyer was either terrorized or (more likely) corrupt.

The other concerned Louis Lepke. By means of a series of legal manoeuvres and appeals, he managed to stay out of the chair until March 1944. In the weeks before his death, there was, however, intense speculation that (in the words of the *New York Mirror*) "Lepke offered material to Governor Dewey that would make him an unbeatable

BELOW
Rose Reles, the widow of "Kid Twist" Reles, hides her face in grief at the funeral of her husband. Many members of Murder, Inc., also came to regret the whole Reles incident.

presidential candidate" if he used it.

It was widely understood that he was not referring to Mob secrets, but to the career of Sidney Hillman, at that time President of the Amalgamated Clothing Workers Union and President Roosevelt's principal labour adviser. The problem, from Lepke's standpoint, was that he was asking too much in return: not only his own life, but (in effect) a blank sheet for organized crime in the United States. Another way of looking at it is to say that he was offering Dewey the presidency of the United States – essentially a personal bribe – in return for dropping literally hundreds of potential murder investigations. Even presidential candidates realize that there are limits to the gullibility of the electorate, and Dewey knew that if he let that deal go down, he would be marked as the most repulsively cynical man ever to have a serious chance at the White House.

In the event, the deal did not work. Louis Capone, Mendy Weiss and then Louis Lepke were executed in the chair within minutes of one another. Others who suffered the same fate, as a

result of "the canary who could sing but couldn't fly", were Pittsburg Phil, Buggsy Goldstein, Happy Maione and Dasher Abbandando. "Gurrah" Shapiro had been jailed years before, in 1936, and ended his days in prison in 1947, at the age of 48. He had been in favour of killing Dewey, too, but he was not high enough up the Mafia tree for his voice to count and, to the end, he was convinced (perhaps justifiably) that they should have "whacked" him.

Although Murder, Inc. was not out of business in its original form, the need for the same kind of services continued. The only difference was that the business was now decentralized. In a number of communities scattered throughout the country,

ABOVE
Sidney Hillman, principal labour adviser to President Roosevelt. Lepke's offer of mob secrets that would ruin Hillman – and by association Roosevelt – was turned down by Governor Dewey.

there are houses that are neither abandoned nor apparently lived in. Their owners do the bare minimum of exterior maintenance, and although there are never lights at the windows, there are sometimes cars parked nearby. In order to gain admission, a complex series of knocks or rings is required. If you could get inside, you would find a bar, maybe a workout room, a couple of games rooms, a kitchen, a place to eat, maybe even a couple of rooms with beds in. Slightly sullen, but nonetheless warily polite young men would be hanging around, reading comic books, drinking, shooting the breeze. There might even be a couple of girlfriends there. You would be in a Mafia hit-men's rendezvous.

THE BENEFITS OF WAR

In the last chapter I said that World War II was a time of mixed fortunes for the Mafia. Louis Lepke and his hit men from Murder, Inc., certainly came out badly, but a number of others did rather well. During World War II Meyer Lansky further consolidated his fortunes, Lucky Luciano came out of jail, and some members of the Mafia managed to involve themselves with American intelligence and military forces, and with what was to become the CIA.

In time of war, the need for booze, betting and broads does not diminish. Those soldiers who are fortunate enough to get home are always good customers, although some may expect to be treated to booze and broads. The American economy as a whole boomed during the war, as the government spent money like water and the wealth of the British Empire poured into the United States, the arms supplier to the Allies. Most people who were not fighting – and the American forces, with such a huge labour reserve, could afford to be selective about who they took in – had more money in their pockets than ever before. Machinists found themselves in the middle of a bonanza and, because so many men were away fighting, a large number of women entered the labour market for the first time. Many of them, no doubt, did so to make ends meet while their menfolk were away fighting, while others spent their earnings on themselves, either because they had no attachments or because they repudiated

ABOVE
During World War II, many women entered the labour market to undertake jobs that had previously been the preserve of men.

LEFT
Women workers, wearing safety glasses, test .30 calibre ammunition on an arms company indoor firing range in 1943.

them. There were also many women who suddenly found themselves to be part of a two-income family, with their partners even more handsomely paid than themselves.

In addition to supplying traditional pleasures to a newly affluent society, intelligent mobsters also found that there were some things that could be sold on the black market, even in the affluent United States. With European markets very effectively closed, anyone who could beg, steal, borrow or re-create European-style luxuries could be sure of handsome profits. Not only luxury items, but such staples as sugar and the all-American drug of choice, coffee, were also in short supply, as well as butter, shoes, tyres for motor cars – all kinds of everyday things.

Although some luxuries might literally be unobtainable at times, there was always the possibility of finding a cache somewhere, with or without the consent of the original owner or the knowledge of US customs and excise officials. The most lucrative items, however, were things like sugar and butter. Those who had permission to sell them might find that a Mafia "tax" had to be paid

to make sure that the goods actually arrived in the shops, and those who did not have permission might find that the goods were available, but only if bought from the right place.

Another fruitful source of income for the Mob was the docks. The country may well be engaged in a great war, but people still had to be paid for loading and unloading, and for trucking. Union regulation meant that the pool of available labour at the docks was restricted. The combination of a seller's market and a small number of sellers provided great opportunities for the Mafia.

That anyone could be so ruthlessly opportunist while others were dying in battle may be repulsive, but it is commonplace in all wars. In many ways, the Mafia were no worse than the high-powered industrialists who owned the munitions companies, and whose fortunes were being increased daily by the war. Goldwater may have popularized the phrase "the military-industrial complex", but the apparatus the phrase symbolized had been in place for decades. However, the depths of cynicism were reached in the sinking of the *Normandie* on 11 February 1942.

BELOW
The scarcity of imported goods and of labour increased the Mafia's hold on the docks, already a traditional site of racketeering.

SABOTAGE AND PATRIOTISM

The SS *Normandie,* recently renamed the *Lafayette,* was one of the fastest and finest of the transatlantic liners of the day. Comfort was not at issue – by the time she was a troop-ship, she would have packed men in like sardines – but speed was: a fast convoy is almost always safer than a slow one.

Luciano was at this time running the Mafia from prison, but his style was somewhat cramped by conditions at Dannemora, one of the hardest prisons in the New York system. He already knew that Federal authorities were paranoid about dock workers of German and Italian descent, whom they believed (probably inaccurately) were sending signals to enemy submarines offshore. However, perhaps surprisingly, in view of his general reputation for lack of intellect, it was Albert Anastasia of Murder, Inc. who first saw an opportunity in this. Neither the Feds nor the New York Police Department had much influence or control in the docks and shipyards, but the Mob did. If the Mob volunteered to help the government, the government would owe the Mob

a favour, which might be negotiated into an early release for Luciano. Anastasia suggested the idea to Lansky, who gave the go-ahead.

In order to emphasize the risk of enemy agents running amok in the docks, Albert Anastasia's brother "Tough Tony" Anastasio (different spelling) then arranged to have the *Normandie* burned. Apparently, as a former Army sergeant, Anastasia loved the idea of giving the Navy a poke in the eye, so the sinking was a labour of love as much as a Mob job.

Although they put out an anodyne statement that the fire could have been due to "worker carelessness", the Federal government knew full well that it was sabotage. They therefore promptly launched "Operation Underworld", asking Joseph "Socks" Lanza what could be arranged. "Socks" was the head of the fish-market racket. He was a big enough man to be known to the authorities, but not a big enough problem to warrant action by them. He passed them on to Frank Costello and Meyer Lansky, who in turn assured the Navy men who were making the contact that only Luciano had the power to arrange things. Luciano agreed to use his influence.

⊕

RIGHT
The *Lafayette* (*Normandie*) burns at a New York quay, sabotaged by the Mafia in 1942.

⊕

LEFT
The US government initially contacted Joseph "Socks" Lanza, (pictured here) a known mobster, in their bid to enlist the Mafia's help in dealing with "Nazi" activity at the docks.

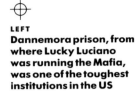

LEFT
Dannemora prison, from where Lucky Luciano was running the Mafia, was one of the toughest institutions in the US prison system.

LEFT
Great Meadow prison, considerably more comfortable than Dannemora, to which Luciano was transferred after negotiations following the *Normandie* (*Lafayette*) incident.

By an extraordinary coincidence, "Nazi" activity on the docks ceased forthwith. Luciano was transferred from Dannemora prison to the much more comfortable Great Meadow; and just after the war, Governor Dewey arranged for Luciano to be released on parole on the grounds of his patriotic services to the country.

With the benefit of hindsight, the Mafia's ploy seems obvious. At the time, however, the overall level of paranoia was running at a very high level,

and it was simply easier to believe in outside machinations by Hitler and his Nazis than it was to accept that the government was being manipulated by organized crime. The American people have always preferred outside enemies to inside ones. The Kefauver investigations into the Mob had considerable impact, but they would pale beside McCarthy's investigations into communism. The "Commie Threat" came from without, but organized crime was mainly a domestic problem.

THE INVASION
OF SICILY

The *Normandie* incident was not the only involvement of high-level government with the Mob. As World War II ground to an end, and the invasion of Sicily was planned, the Mafia were enlisted there too.

The details of this remain even shadowier than the details of the *Normandie* affair, which was described in the posthumous memoirs of Luciano, and confirmed by interviews in Israel with Lansky. It seems, though, that the Mob not only supplied people who knew the invasion sites like the backs of their hands, but also offered all sorts of inside contacts in Sicily: men who could identify collaborators, root out former Fascist officials, describe the best ways through the mountains, point out the weaknesses of enemy positions, the locations of secret headquarters and more.

The morass of loyalties is bewildering. Many Sicilians never saw themselves as Italian anyway and the Mafia was of course against Mussolini's men because of his anti-Mafia stand. The Mob presumably behaved as they had behaved in the burning of the *Normandie,* putting personal and tribal interests above national loyalties (whether American, Italian or Sicilian). The net result was that a number of highly placed government and army officials either owed favours to the Mafia, or thought they did.

LUCIANO IN
EXILE

Although Luciano was released in 1946, he was also deported to Italy. Whether in acknowledgment that he might not be popular there, or simply to be nearer where the action was, Luciano was in Cuba within the year. When the US government found out where he was, they successfully forced the Cuban government to expel him back to Italy by the simple, if ruthless, expedient of threatening to interdict all imports of legitimate pharmaceuticals to Cuba. From his native land, Luciano continued to run the Mob for almost a decade before his power started to wane. Both he and Lansky would remain powers to be reckoned with in the 1950s, as we shall see in the next chapter.

ABOVE
Lucky Luciano relaxes at his home in Naples, Italy. Although deported more than ten years before this photograph was taken in 1958, Luciano was still influential in the US Mafia.

IT'S ONLY BUSINESS

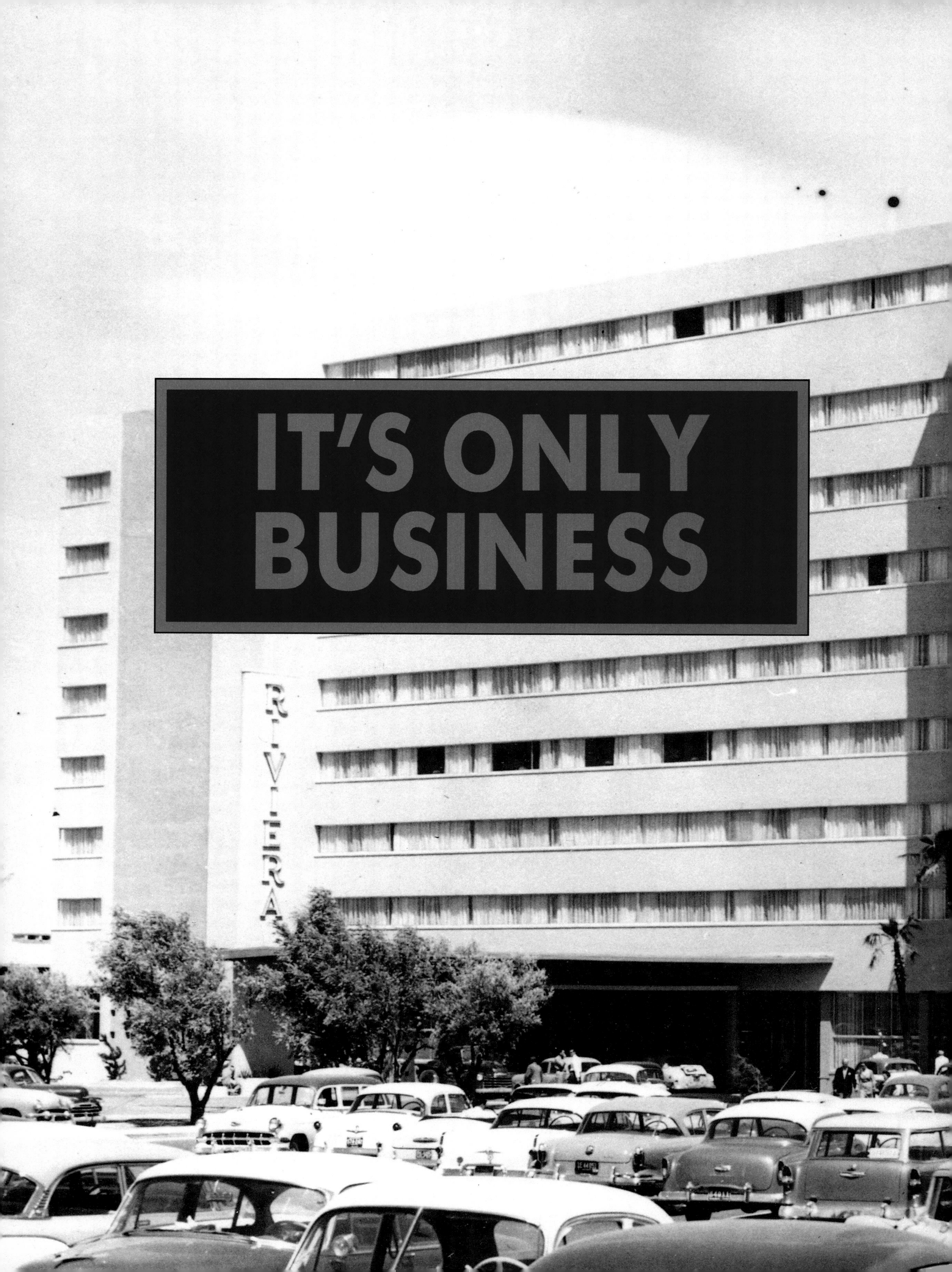

THERE IS A PERSISTENT rumour that "real" mafiosi refuse to get involved in drugs. The proponents of the "Honourable Society" concept of the Mafia sometimes argue that drugs are inconsistent with *omertà*.

It might conceivably be true that there are Men of Honour who will not soil their hands with drugs. Although why drugs are so much worse than, for instance, white-slaving or "buckwheat" murders is not something that is easy to explain. In any case, even if the most principled mafiosi refuse to deal in drugs, there are plenty of others in organized crime (to say nothing of the less principled mafiosi) who are more than willing to deal in coke, heroin, crack or whatever. The money involved is so staggering that it is almost inconceivable that they should not.

DRUG PROFITS

At the time of writing, there had been several busts of ten tons or more of cocaine. A ton of cocaine (2240 lb or 2000 lb, depending on whether you use imperial or short measure) is close enough to a tonne (1000 kg or 2200 lb). A kilo of coke, wholesale, has fluctuated between $12,500 and $50,000 for some years; a tonne, therefore, is worth $12,500,000 to $50,000,000.

These figures are much more meaningful than the inflated "street prices" that are often quoted in the media. On the street, the dope is often "cut" with adulterants, and a gram ($\frac{1}{25}$ oz) of coke costing maybe $50 to $100 might be no more than 50 per cent pure. At these rates, a single kilo is worth anything from $50,000 to $200,000, depending on purity. This means that tens of millions can be made from just one tonne. A gram is roughly equivalent to five lines, one line being a normal dose.

What is more, the cost of producing the stuff is not all that high: it is in the tens of dollars per kilo, certainly no more than a few hundred dollars a kilo even after allowing for all overheads. Nor is it expensive to ship: a small aeroplane can carry half a tonne (ten or 20 million dollars' worth). You can buy such an aircraft for well under $50,000. The only risk lies in the smuggling and distribution; exactly the fields in which organized crime might be expected to excel.

The demand for cocaine in the United States is roughly several hundred tonnes a year – the biggest single market. As the saying goes, "Cocaine is God's way of telling you that you have too much money". Even if you lose aircraft, pilots, and a few tonnes of cocaine, the profits will easily make good the losses. This is a business that runs into the tens or even hundreds of billions of dollars a year; it may even break the trillion-a-year barrier – and

that's just cocaine. Most heroin addicts require a minimum 50 mg per day. One US government estimate – widely regarded as optimistically low – puts the number of heroin addicts at 100,000. Multiply 100,000 users by 50 mg per day, and you have five kilos a day. The wholesale rate for heroin is in excess of $250,000 a kilo. The street price could easily go as high as $100 for a day's habit, or $2 million a kilo. Remember, that's for a product where the total import only has to run at 5 to 10 kilos a day. A single condom, carried in the vagina

BELOW
Customs agents unload some of a large shipment of cocaine, seized off Key West from the vessel in the background.

ABOVE
An agent weighs
packages of cocaine as
other agents carry
planks to a saw to be cut
open. The planks are
hollow to conceal the
cocaine.

RIGHT
Despite the successes of
the authorities, large
amounts of drugs get
through. Here an addict
surreptitiously injects
himself with his
favoured "fix".

of a courier, can hold as much as 100 g, with a potential value of $30,000 at wholesale rates. A false bottom in a suitcase can easily carry a couple of kilos, which may be worth $500,000. This is a business where the numbers run to $10 to $20 million *a day* in the United States.

Then there is marijuana. If it were taxed at $1,000,000 a tonne, the street price would still have room to fall. Many hundreds, or maybe several thousands of tonnes of weed go up in smoke every year. Even at a modest $1000 a kilo, a thousand tonnes of marijuana is a billion dollars.

Then there are uppers, downers, "angel dust", acid – you name it someone is probably hooked on it, psychologically if not physiologically. People have always taken whatever drugs they could afford: in Glasgow in the 1920s, they would even drink milk that had had coal gas bubbled through it, for a cheap high.

It is not difficult to see, therefore, that the profits in drugs are potentially, and often in reality, disturbingly titanic.

THE GROWTH OF THE DRUG PROBLEM

As early as the 1920s, or even before, there had been some Mob involvement in narcotics shipping; it is easy to forget, or not always remember, that cocaine was nearly as much the drug of choice for the "beautiful people" of the 1920s as it was for those of the 1980s. For many years, though, narcotics prosecutions were not a high priority. Even at the lower prices then offered, few people could afford the luxury of drugs other than alcohol, caffeine and nicotine. Then, as society became more affluent, it became possible to sell more drugs. Cocaine is perhaps the ultimate vindication of "supply-side" economics: the market seems literally limitless.

In truth, there were other factors at work as well. Not only did J. Edgar Hoover deny the existence of the Mafia, but he also tried as far as possible to keep the FBI out of drug enforcement. He may have foreseen (quite accurately) that even G-men would be susceptible to bribery by drug barons, because there was so much money around. It is extremely likely that lax enforcement meant

that there was a very significant drug problem perhaps as early as the 1930s or 1940s, and certainly by the 1950s.

Even in 1960, a kilo of Marseilles heroin cost about $2,500 in France and was worth about three times as much in New York, traditionally the point of entry for the vast majority of heroin to the United States. Properly cut with lactose (for bulk) and quinine (to give the characteristic bitter taste), a kilo would provide an addict with a 20,000 days' supply, or alternatively 10 days' supply for 2000 addicts. In that form, it would be worth anything from $200,000 to $600,000 on the street. Twenty years later, the cost in Marseilles (or in Palermo, which also had its share of "cooks" or drug chemists) had gone up fivefold, but the wholesale price in New York had gone up by a factor of 40. This reflected two things: greatly increased demand, and greatly increased risk.

The majority of Americans first became aware of drugs in the mid-1960s. The better informed had known about them for much longer, but the explosion of the "counter-culture" in the 1960s brought new words into the vocabulary of people who might never dream of using drugs, but who read about them almost daily in their newspapers. The media blitz was extraordinary, and could be

LEFT
Drugs are nothing new. Here a waterfront junkie injects seamen with morphine in the 1920s.

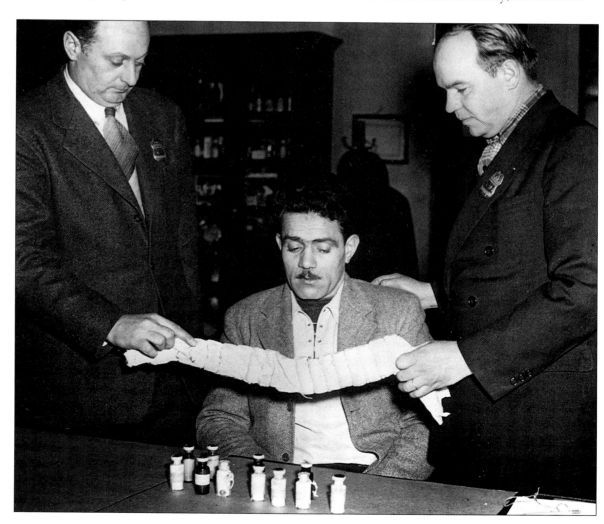

RIGHT
A ship's machinist after his arrest for attempted drug smuggling in 1948. The agents hold the waistband in which the drugs were concealed.

divided in two parts: a small but vociferous pro-drug lobby, largely in the "alternative" press, and a much larger (and frequently far less well-informed) anti-drug lobby.

Regardless of the actual dangers of drugs, which were without question significant enough, there were strong motives to paint them as still worse than they were. The "American Century" had really only begun at the end of 1947, when Indian independence signalled the end of the British Empire and indicated that, regardless of her history, Britain was unlikely to regain super-power status, at least in the twentieth century. The 1950s were a time of unparalleled affluence in the United States, both in absolute terms and (perhaps still more importantly) in relative terms when compared with the European economies. However, with the assassination of John F. Kennedy in 1963, the American Century appeared to be tottering. Even to a nation so accustomed to doing things quickly, a century that lasted less than two decades looked unpromising. Drugs provided a wonderful scapegoat for some, and a means of escape for others. Demagogues could blame just about anything they liked on "the drug problem" (they still do), and this meant that the police were under heavy pressure to catch drug dealers so that they could show that something was being done.

ABOVE
Vito Genovese, the best known Mafia Boss to be heavily involved in the "unAmerican activity" of drug trading. He is pictured here being returned to America in 1945.

AN
UNAMERICAN
ACTIVITY

This was the origin of the so-called "No Narcotics" rule of the Mafia. Regular organized crime, with its murders and extortion rackets and white-slaving and union racketeering, was something that the establishment had come to terms with. It was, after all, only *laissez-faire* capitalism in its purest form. Drugs, on the other hand, represented a threat to the American Way of Life; so drug investigations were pursued with the kind of vigour that the Mob found very unwelcome. It is entirely likely that some Bosses refused to deal in drugs personally, simply because they had no need to do so; but there is no doubt that many underbosses, Capos, Soldiers and hangers-on were heavily involved in the drugs trade, as were some of the Bosses. Those few Bosses who genuinely did forbid drug dealing, and either paid an extra salary to compensate for lost earnings (as did Frank Accardo in Chicago) or simply "hit" disobedient Soldiers, did so mainly out of self preservation. A successful drug investigation might have consequences that were altogether too far-reaching.

"DON" VITO GENOVESE

The best-known of the Bosses to be involved in the drug trade was Vito Genovese, though it seems likely that the deal for which he was most famous was not even of his own making. It was part of an elaborate set-up that was designed to thwart his attempt to revive the old post of *Capo di Tutti Capi,* with himself as the star.

Genovese was born in 1897, and was a sidekick to Lucky Luciano in the 1920s, but by 1937 – when already 40 – he ran into trouble on a murder rap and fled to Italy. There, by an extraordinary combination of charm and commercial acumen, he managed to ingratiate himself with Mussolini. Not least among his advantages to Mussolini was that he oversaw the supply of clean, reliable drugs to Count Ciano, Mussolini's son-in-law and Italy's foreign minister. This, incidentally, was not an

unusual aberration among Fascist leaders. Hermann Goering is reputed to have used cocaine enthusiastically, whatever the Führer might have said about "degenerate Jews and jungle blacks" being the only users of such stuff in his Fascist paradise.

During the war, Genovese organized the assassination of Carlo Tresca, an anti-Fascist newspaperman who had taken refuge in New York. Tresca was shot in the head by Carmine Galante, who would in three decades' time become the leader of the Bonanno family in New York. Then, at the end of the war, "Don" Vito (as he liked to be called) switched allegiance with remarkable facility and became an interpreter for invading US forces in Italy.

At first, the American army could hardly believe its luck. Their new interpreter was well connected, and he even helped them to break some of the black market rackets, which were endemic in Italy

BELOW
Carlo Tresca, the Italian anti-fascist and labour leader, here speaking in New York in 1927. His assassination during World War II was organized by Vito Genovese.

in the aftermath of the war. Then they found out that when it came to running a black market, Genovese could teach any of their petty criminals a great deal; and he was arrested and returned to the United States for his old murder charge.

Fortunately for Genovese, all the witnesses against him came down with "Sicilian Flu", which in some cases apparently proved fatal. He was not convicted, and not only did he regain his freedom, but he was not even deported. He now had major-league ambitions for power in the American Mafia.

For years, he worked assiduously to build his power base, but not until 1957 did he feel strong enough to attempt to "hit" Frank Costello, still one of the most important men in the Mob. The attempt failed – Costello would not die until 1973, of natural causes and over the age of 80 – but it put him on notice that Genovese was a man to worry about. A few months after the attempt on

RIGHT
Vito Genovese, smiling broadly, arrives in court for a hearing in 1959, a year after being convicted for being the mastermind of an international narcotics ring.

BELOW
Philip Kennedy, who was with Costello just before he was shot by Genovese's men, arrives at the police station. While inside, Kennedy's office received a death threat against Kennedy should he talk.

Costello's life, Genovese's men successfully took out Albert Anastasia in a barber's chair at the Park Sheraton Hotel in New York, and Costello apparently hatched two plans. One was to retire and the other was to set up Vito Genovese so that he would go down for a good, long time.

In order to achieve the latter, he enlisted the help of a number of Mafia "Dons", including Meyer Lansky and Lucky Luciano. First, they put together a handsome narcotics smuggling deal, and then they paid a Puerto Rican drug smuggler, called Nelson Cantellops, $100,000 to "sing" to the police. As a result of Cantellops's efforts, Genovese went down for 15 years in 1959 when he was 62 years old. The actual case was apparently very shaky, but the prosecutors decided to ignore some of the more dubious areas of the evidence and take what they had been handed. A decade later, Genovese died in prison.

NOT A MAFIA
MONOPOLY

It is also worth adding that as far as anyone can tell, a great deal of the drug trade outside the United States (including bringing it into the country) is conducted without the assistance of the Mafia. The famous "French Connection" of the 1960s was apparently planned by old-time French gangs from Marseilles, with the Mafia end merely the most useful way to handle the stuff in the United States. The French have a strong tradition of organized crime of their own, with Paris and Marseilles the equivalents of New York and Chicago, and raw opium came either from former colonies in French Indo-China or from Turkey. The juice of the opium poppy has always been gathered by hand and either sun-dried or artificially dried to form a brown, sticky mass, in which form it was eaten or smoked by the opium-lovers of old. For the French Connection, the raw opium was traditionally shipped to the Lebanon for processing into a morphine base, which was in turn reprocessed in Marseilles to give diacetylmorphine hydrochloride – heroin. There may, however, now be a major Sicilian (and therefore Mafia) connection for heroin, because French "cooks" are reputed to have taken their expertise to Sicily after the destruction of the "French Connection".

The Medellin cartel, of cocaine fame, likewise developed with the very minimum of assistance from the Mob. Actually growing marijuana, or importing the rather bulky bales that are necessary

to meet demand, is a bit too much like hard work for the Mob.

Once the drugs are inside the United States, it is again debatable whether the Mafia is really crucial to their distribution, although they almost certainly take "protection money" from those who actually sell the stuff. The Hell's Angels and other motorcycle gangs are often cited as major distributors, though this may be as much a journalistic invention as a real phenomenon. Often, too, various Hispanic gangs (Cuban, Colombian, Puerto Rican and Mexican) are blamed for "pushing". Then there is "ethnic succession in

ABOVE
The risks of the drugs trade are high, but the amount of money involved gives profits to match.

RIGHT
Minority groups or subcultures – such as these Hell's Angels pictured in 1966 – are often blamed, whether rightly or wrongly, by the general public for the drug problems in society.

LEFT
An attempt by any one organization to have complete control of the drugs trade would be like trying to achieve a monopoly in any other commodity. Here agents in Peru hold four suspects from a South American drugs organization.

RIGHT
The broken paraphernalia of a confirmed drug user.

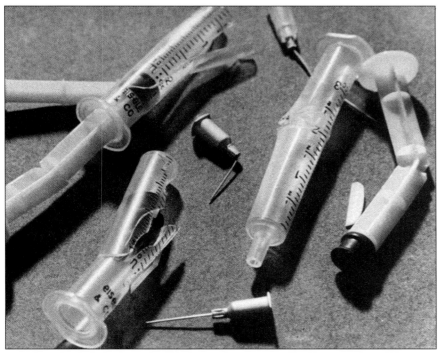

organized crime", the "black Mafia", lately supplemented by horror stories of West Indian gangs. Other candidates include the Yakuza (Japanese "Mafia"), other Oriental gangs from Vietnam and Laos, and the long-suffering CIA.

The truth is probably that the sheer volume of drugs that are distributed in America is such that it is impractical for the Mob to have any more than local control; it would be like trying to establish a national monopoly for sugar, or for timber. The various journalistic "revelations" depend to a large extent on the orientation of the journalist, and on his intended audience. Many Americans do not like motorcyclists, therefore "motorcycle gangs" are a good target. There is a strong redneck audience who wants to hear racist attacks, so Hispanics, blacks or Orientals are a good bet. Any 1960s-style liberal, brought up on "Hey! Hey! LBJ! How many kids did you kill today?" is more than willing to believe that the government is capable of anything, so there is another easy target.

ABOVE
Roulette in Las Vegas, Nevada, 1950s.

THE GAMBLING
BUSINESS

There is much less doubt, though, about Mafia involvement in casinos; and the classic locations were Las Vegas in Nevada, and Fulgencio Batista's Cuba. The great advantage of both was that gambling there was "legal".

The reason that "legal" is in quotation marks is that there are degrees of legality in gambling. Although it is perfectly possible to run an absolutely straight, legal, honest and above-board casino, it usually does not happen. There are just too many opportunities for cheating. After all, gambling depends on cash, and cash is wonderfully untraceable stuff. It's not even

necessary to cheat the gamblers: you can cheat the owners, and you can also cheat the tax-man.

Cheating the gamblers is only worthwhile with the high-rollers, the ones who habitually gamble thousands and who are good for tens of thousands or even hundreds of thousands. Even then, you do not want to cheat them too badly, or they won't come back. Regardless of what they say, most gamblers are secretly reconciled to losing, and even if they lose a little more than they expected they live with it. Stacked decks, mirrors, hidden TV cameras, rigged roulette wheels, loaded or "shaved" dice: all of these and more have been, and no doubt still are, used.

It is also worth adding that there are an awful lot of gamblers who are totally incompetent.

Watch a professional blackjack player, and you will see that he (or she) bets methodically, increasing bets until a losing hand turns up, then regressing to a base-level bet. Blackjack is probably the only casino game where a skilled, card-counting player can enjoy an advantage over the house. Then watch a typical amateur. They win five dollars; bet 50; lose that; lose their nerve; go back to betting five; lose fives a couple of times; win a couple of fives; then bet 50 again because they think they are "on a roll". With people like these around, the casino has no need to be dishonest.

Cheating the owners is more profitable. It is inherent in the nature of a casino that the odds favour the house; they could not stay in business otherwise. Even a "straight" game should ensure that the house takes anything upwards of about two-and-a-half per cent of the total turnover; sometimes more, but rarely less. In a country where gambling is strictly controlled, so that people have only a limited number of places where they can go to gamble, you can rely on an enormous volume of trade. This is of course the traditional situation in the United States.

The classic way to cheat the owners is the "skim". No one keeps written records of each hand (or spin of the wheel, or roll of the dice) or of how much is taken in. Before the money goes into the owners' pockets it is easy to "skim" anything from 10 to 50 per cent of the takings.

The trouble with cheating the owners arises when the owners catch you. With normal civil penalties – fines and jail – you may be prepared to take the risk. When the penalty is being suspended on a meat-hook through the rectum and then being tortured with an electric cattle prod, to say nothing of having your testicles crushed with pliers, you may be more inclined to think twice. This is one of several areas where a ruthless or crooked casino owner has a major advantage over one who stays within the law.

Cheating the tax man is where the major profits are. Again, it's a "skim", but this time, the owners are the ones who do the skimming. The other great advantage of cheating the tax man is that no one really regards it as a crime, especially in the United States where cheating the tax man is almost as much a national sport as it is in Italy.

BELOW
Gambling in a Las Vegas casino, 1960s.

THE BIRTH OF LAS VEGAS

For more than four decades, from 1931 onwards, Nevada was the only American state where gambling was legal. In 1941, El Rancho Vegas was already a well-established luxury hotel-casino on Highway 91, which would later be re-christened "The Strip". In 1942, the Last Frontier was also built on the 91. Neither seems to have been run by a scion of organized crime. The same is true of the other gambling hotels downtown, but in 1945 Bugsy Siegel bought into El Cortez, a downtown establishment, using his own money and that of a number of friends, including Meyer Lansky.

Contrary to popular belief, Lansky does not seem to have been the driving force behind the Mob's getting into Las Vegas. He already had his own perfectly successful "carpet joints" (illegal casino/restaurants) in Florida, and he had a low opinion of the future of Las Vegas. The $60,000 that he invested was a 10 per cent stake, and he seems to have been a sleeping partner. Bugsy Siegel appears to have been the real driving force.

El Cortez was sold in July 1946 at a profit of $166,000, and the money was to be re-invested in the Flamingo. This was an all-new, all-glitz project from Billy Wilkerson, who had founded the *Hollywood Reporter* as well as the Café Trocadero, Ciro's and La Rue's on the "other" strip, in Hollywood. Wilkerson's money ran out, though, and the whole $650,000 from the sale of El Cortez was applied to buy a two-thirds share of the project.

The concept of the Flamingo was great: a Beverly Hills ambience to replace the "dude ranch" ambience of the existing resort casinos. The initial experience was however a disaster. Cost overruns were enormous, and when the casino opened at Christmas 1946 the hotel was not yet ready, so the real losers – the ones who gambled late into the night after they had eaten, while their wives went to bed – lost their money elsewhere, at the casino/hotels where they were staying. It was widely believed that Bugsy had creamed off a good deal of construction money, and more money had to be raised. This time it came from Frank Costello and Meyer Lansky. The new casino closed again at the end of January 1947, and remained closed until 1 March, when it re-opened complete with hotel. On 20 June, Bugsy was shot at short range with a .30 army carbine while he was reading the Los Angeles *Times* at the home of his girlfriend Virginia Hill: he was "whacked" so efficiently that his right eye was blown 15 feet from his body by the impact of the shots.

According to one version, Virginia Hill was the original "Flamingo" who lent her name to the project, and by her own testimony, she had considerable sexual talents. The latter was the explanation she gave to the Kefauver commission when they pressed her on why so many men had given her so much money. At the time of the killing, she was elsewhere. She and Bugsy had had one of their periodical rows, and she had gone to Paris via Chicago and New York.

Lansky probably had nothing to do with it. The people who paid for the hit were almost certainly Siegel's associates who were unhappy about being ripped off. By his death, which (with appropriately gory pictures) made the front cover of just about every newspaper in America, Benjamin Siegel brought the relationship between the Mob and Las Vegas to the fore.

RIGHT
Virginia Hill, the girlfriend of Bugsy Siegal, is rumoured to have been the original "Flamingo" after whom the casino was named.

A MAFIA TOWN

The exact ownership of the other casinos is necessarily hazy. The Las Vegas gaming control authorities could and sometimes did refuse licenses to casinos which were known to have links with the Mob, so "front men" were employed all over the place. It is widely believed (and still more widely reported) that the Sands was backed by Meyer Lansky, Joe Adonis, Frank Costello and Doc Stacher; the Thunderbird was primarily a Lansky operation; the Desert Inn belonged to Moe Dalitz and the Cleveland Mob; the Sahara and the Riviera were financed by Tony Accardo ("Joe Batters"), Sam Giancana and the Fischetti brothers; and Raymond Patriarca was the man behind the Dunes. Frank Costello and Dandy Phil Castell apparently owned the Tropicana, while Caesar's Palace is aptly described by Mafia historian Carl Sifakis as having attracted a "Roman legion of Mafia investors".

What further confuses the ownership of the various casino-hotels is the interlocking financial structure of the whole city. Typically, a big investor might have five "points" (per cent) here, 12½ "points" there, and 30 "points" somewhere else. Some people consider this financial labyrinth, attributed to Meyer Lansky, as being a means of avoiding gang wars over territory, but more likely it reflects the *ad hoc* nature of "organized" crime. I'll see you OK here, if you'll cut me in on that, and hey, we both owe Joe Batters a favour and wouldn't it be a good idea to cut Meyer Lansky in because everyone knows he runs a straight house. Add to this the complex nature of Mafia inheritances, and it is soon clear that no deep-laid plans are needed, because the financial structures will fall into place.

Mafia inheritances, needless to say, do not usually depend on family relations, but on Family status. Wives, honest sons, girlfriends all have the potential to ruin a smooth-running deal. Normally, the family is taken care of by the Family, who may inherit by simple murder (as when one Boss takes over from another), by a feudal division of spoils, or by a division of a deceased partner's share among his surviving co-investors.

However, at times it may not be clear who the "inheritors" are. For instance, it is likely that Jimmy Hoffa was "whacked" either by the Mob or his fellow teamsters because he was not entirely honest with the Teamsters' pension fund. Ten million dollars is reputed to have gone into Caesar's Palace, maybe one-fifth of the "loans" that the Teamsters Union put into the City of the Stars. Who owns those investments?

Regardless of these complications, the paradoxical effect of having the Mob in Las Vegas

was that it became one of the safest and best-run cities in the United States (it remains one of the safest to this day). Because it depended effectively on tourism – a gambler is merely a particular kind of tourist, after all – the Mob could see that confidence in Las Vegas was the beginning and end of their prosperity. As long as people believed that they could go to Las Vegas and gamble against known odds (even if those odds favoured the house, as they always do), and be able to take their winnings away without fear of hindrance, they were going to keep on coming. Never was Bugsy Siegel's line that "We only kill each other" more important.

Throughout the 1950s, Las Vegas became more and more important and successful. Air travel into the city became quicker, cheaper and more comfortable. The "sun belt" and (in particular) the explosive growth of California provided an ever-larger pool of potential gamblers. No longer was Eastern money the main source of revenue. Increased affluence meant that the casinos could also make their money on the volume of trade: a few tens or hundreds of dollars from thousands of small players, rather than taking thousands or tens of thousands from a handful of high rollers. The

ABOVE
Frank Costello, just one of the many mobsters involved in Las Vegas. He was in near the start when he became involved with the Flamingo, and then later when he apparently co-owned the Tropicana.

RIGHT
One of the first photographs of the Desert Inn in its original form. It opened its doors in 1950, and was owned by Moe Dalitz and the Cleveland Mob.

LEFT
The front entrance of Dunes in 1955, a giant statue of an Arabian shiek mounted on the roof. The casino had the backing of Raymond Patriarca.

old "carpet houses" on the outskirts of almost all major cities, which were the spiritual successors to the speakeasies that had died with prohibition, were steadily being closed down by an increasingly moralistic America.

The profits from these commercial opportunities were greater than the Mob was used to. It was time for legitimate business to move in. In the 1960s, Howard Hughes started buying up the casinos. This was a dream for the older generation of gangsters, because it provided them with absolutely "clean" money with which to retire; or if they wished, of course, to re-invest elsewhere. Because of skimming, though, Hughes never saw quite as much money as he expected: he was looking for 20 per cent return on his investment, and he apparently saw more like six. By 1970 he was several million dollars in the hole, at which point it seems that the Mob bought their way back in to Las Vegas. In the 1980s, this was to lead to a whole new round of gang wars, but this is material for the next chapter.

C U B A

From the very beginning, Cuba must in any case have looked like a much easier place to run a casino than Las Vegas. Not only was it more convenient for siphoning off the money of the Eastern United States, but the climate was more agreeable. Its prices and taxes were lower, and nobody paid much attention to the little law there was. If you wanted to get your underage whore drunk, no problem. If someone cut up rough about a rigged game, he would find the police strangely unsympathetic. If the odds were not quite the ones that you expected, well, go play somewhere else. Both Cuban and *Norteamericano* dealers cheated merrily, typically at multidice games such as cubolo and razzle-dazzle.

The Mafia – or, more precisely, Meyer Lansky – actually cleaned the place up, for much the same reasons as they made Las Vegas a safe place for the punters. After Fulgencio Batista had regained power in March 1952, he requested Lansky to act as a "consultant" on gaming in Cuba at a fee of $25,000 a year (perhaps $100,000 to $150,000 in modern terms). Batista saw perfectly well that in order to attract and keep gamblers, the games had to be reasonably "clean". That is, the odds had to be fairly honest. In the early 1950s, they definitely were not. The tables at some casinos were

ABOVE
The cashier at a Havana casino in 1940. Many American dollars have found their way into the safe behind him.

LEFT
The baccarat room of the Casino Nacional in Havana, Cuba. At the time of this picture, 1929, the casino was regarded as the world's most elaborate.

ABOVE RIGHT
The casino in the Riviera Hotel, Havana where American gamblers would both stay and play the tables.

RIGHT
Croupiers at a Havana casino looking almost sinister as they wait for their game of chance to lure gamblers and their money.

apparently rented out on a table-by-table basis, and inevitably, some of the renters were fly-by-nights, or ran rigged games. There were only a few "straight" casinos, such as the one that Santo Trafficante Jr. had been running since 1946. His father, Santo Trafficante Sr., was the numbers boss of Tampa in Florida.

Initially, Lansky ran the top-of-the-market Montmartre Club in partnership with its Cuban owners, but soon the Hotel Nacional was equipped with a casino, with Meyer's brother Jake in charge of credit control. By 1956, Meyer was planning to build his own hotel, the Riviera. It actually opened on the evening of 10 December, 1957, with Ginger Rogers as the keynote entertainer, and a first-class restaurant so that the high-rollers could take a break for a world-class meal and then return to the serious business of losing money. Prostitutes were rigorously excluded from the casino, restaurant and bars, unless they were already escorted by a paying customer (in which case they weren't whores, they were "escorts"). Cuba was America's playground.

C A S T R O   A N D
T H E   C I A

The problem was, the money was not being spread around equitably enough. In particular, the lowest classes of Cuban society were getting nothing unless they worked in the casinos, or unless they were spectacularly beautiful teenage girls who could sell their bodies in the Casa Marina. For the right price, a tourist could buy a virgin of 13 or maybe even younger. Of course, the ever-moral Lansky had nothing to do with this, but it was the lure of his casinos (and the infrastructure of hotels, restaurants and other legal attractions which they supported) that made the Casa Marina possible.

As early as 1956, there were those in the Sierra Maestra who had different visions of how Cuba should be ruled, and their ambitions grew with their successes. By the first anniversary of the Riviera's opening, Batista had already applied for US visas for his children. At midnight of the new year of 1959, Batista and his family fled Cuba. Two days later, Ernesto "Che" Guevara led his troops into Havana and on 2 January, Fidel Castro became the prime minister.

Within a few days, the casinos had been shut down. They opened again, briefly, from late February to May 1959, but they showed no profit at that time. Lansky and his associates were out about $5 to $10 million.

In a typically bizarre twist, the CIA now turned to the Mob, which was screaming blue murder about the expropriation of their property in Cuba. Operation Mongoose was a tangled right-wing plot to use Mafia hit men to kill Fidel Castro. Howard Hughes, an ardent anti-communist, is reputed to have been one of the instigators of the idea, via Moe Dalitz. The CIA is supposed to have spent very large sums of money on all kinds of improbable mechanisms for killing Castro – some pure James Bond, others smacking more of Mickey Mouse. They apparently contemplated various ways of poisoning him, including a bacterially infected wet suit, poisoned cigars, and literally a poison pen that was supposed to inject him with some lethal compound. They also considered blowing him up while he was skin-diving. And because respectable governments do not use assassination as a political tool, they hired the Mafia to make the "hit".

ABOVE
President Fulgencio Batista addresses troops in 1952, the year he regained power and asked Meyer Lansky to act as "consultant" on gaming in Cuba.

Hardly anyone in the Mob took things seriously, because the whole idea seemed too farcical. Sam Giancana was the only major Mob figure who may have attempted to do anything for the CIA in return for the large sums of money that they pumped into the Mafia. He was "hit" in 1975 when he was subpoenaed to attend a Senate committee, which might have exposed the whole thing. It is not known if he was hit by the Mob, or by the Company.

KENNEDY

A potentially much bigger political scandal was Kennedy's assassination. In *Mafia Kingfish,* John H. Davis makes a very convincing argument that John F. Kennedy was shot because his brother, Attorney-General Robert Kennedy, was too heavy on the Mafia. Davis traces at least some of that antipathy back to Prohibition, when the fortunes of the Kennedy clan were being consolidated by wise trading in liquor. The President was shot because, in the words of the head of the New Orleans Mafia, the best way to silence a dog's tail is to blow off its head.

However, almost any of the assassination theories is a better one than the official "single gunman" party line, which was propagated after the assassination. Davis has a lot of competition from screwballs, cranks and conspiracy theorists.

There are even those who maintain that Castro put out the contract, in retaliation for Operation Mongoose. Whatever the truth, it demonstrates that as soon as open government fails to hold itself to the very highest standards, it invites comparison with organized crime. Many people joke about this – the IRS (Inland Revenue Service) is often called "the biggest extortion racket in the country", but hard though it may be for the average taxpayer to believe it, the IRS is straight, and wide open to public inspection. The government is not.

ABOVE
23 November 1963, Dallas, Texas. President John F. Kennedy slumps towards his wife after being hit by a sniper's bullet. Were the Mafia involved?

LEFT
Fidel Castro during the March to Havana, which ended in the deposition of Batista. The CIA turned to the Mafia, themselves furious at their losses of assets, in trying to assassinate Castro.

B Y THE 1960S AND 1970S, the Mob was changing considerably. It had started out in the 1920s as a loosely connected club of bootleggers, extortionists and numbers operators. Then, in the 1930s, it had increased considerably in sophistication and cohesiveness, and its focus had switched much more towards gambling. The 1940s saw the growth of the "rackets", essentially an extension of extortion, where in order to get anything done, the Mob had to be paid off. The 1950s were marked by the decline of the old-style "goons", the men who had made their mark by muscle rather than by brains: this change was arguably as great as the change from the old Mafia of the "Mustache Petes" to the organized crime syndicates. In the 1960s, drugs started to be the big money-spinner, but there were many mafiosi who

preferred to stick with semi-legitimate businesses where there was less risk of detection.

This is where the concept of the "Godfather" comes in. As far as can be determined, the application of "Godfather" to the Mafia is purely an invention of Mario Puzo, the author of the famous novel. There is, however, something inherently appropriate about the title. A real godfather, if we have one, is for most of us a shadowy figure of our parents' age who embodies the values of our parents' generation. His influence is rarely great, but we always feel that he has a sort of moral authority in our lives. A Mafia godfather combines that with something akin to the concept of the "fairy godmother", another shadowy figure, but one who has the power to change our lives. A fairy godmother grants our wishes, and can make

ABOVE
A still from Francis Ford Coppola's acclaimed film *The Godfather,* **which was based on Mario Puzo's novel of the same name.**

RIGHT
Mario Puzo, the author of *The Godfather,* **attends the premier of the film of his book in 1972.**

us invulnerable and powerful. A Mafia godfather enjoys that same kind of thrilling power.

A godfather must be a reasonably presentable and well-spoken person who is not obviously a hoodlum. However, he must have the ability to make sure that his wishes are followed, therefore he needs money and influence.

Such a godfather is likely to be found in organized white-collar crime. Strong-arm methods are all very well, but a white-collar criminal can make more money and (in most cases) get away with a smaller sentence if he is unfortunate enough to be caught. Jurors just do not worry as much about large-scale robberies if no one is physically hurt. Combine this with a little old-fashioned muscle, so that you can get the maximum possible return from the bare minimum of violence, and you have the potential for a whole new kind of

mobster. A more intellectual kind of law-breaking, which requires a new kind of "Godfather". Meyer Lansky was the prototype, but Carmine "The Doctor" Lombardozzi was another intellectual "wise guy" from the old school, and John Gotti (born in 1940) was the classic Godfather for the 1980s and 1990s.

NEW STYLE
EXTORTION

Carmine Lombardozzi was born in 1910, and was responsible for a great deal of loan-sharking in the 1950s and probably 1940s. He made initial forays into the stock market, but these were not particularly successful. He and an associate were jailed in 1963 for parole violations associated with earlier stock swindles. His method of operation was, however, elegant.

Young stockbrokers and especially their clerks are often inclined to live beyond their means. There is a certain glamour to the financial life, which is not too different from the glamour of the underworld. If they are courted and "comped" by casinos who treat them like high-rollers, they can quite quickly get into serious financial trouble. The next step is to lend them money at usurious rates, and to point out in a tone of sweetness and light that unless they meet the repayment schedule, they may find themselves with broken legs. Some can get themselves into debt, thereby setting themselves up for equally usurious loans, without even gambling.

In fact, exorbitant interest rates on loans and gambling debts are a great way for the Mafia to get into legitimate business. Even captains of industry can find themselves in the hole to casinos, and a $50,000 debt can easily turn into a 10 per cent share of a business valued at a million dollars. It is up to the Mob then to decide whether they want to stay legit, or whether they want to work (for instance) a "parsley scam".

In the case of indebted finance clerks, it is comparatively easy to induce them either to steal negotiable securities or to be parties to the issue of worthless stocks. Worthless stocks are a particularly fine trick, because there is always the possibility that the people who float them will get away with it. Normally, they do not represent themselves as selling blue-chip stocks. They let it be known that this is a "high risk" stock with the potential of enormous returns, but that it is also one where conventional investors are too stupid to see that the risk is minimal. There are always plenty of people who are convinced that they are smarter than the professionals, and who (in consequence) lose large sums of money.

LEFT
John Gotti was the classic godfather of the 1980s and 1990s. Here, in his expensive suit, he looks more like a company president than most people's idea of a hoodlum.

RIGHT
Meyer Lansky was perhaps the prototype godfather, the first of a breed of more intellectual mobsters.

At this point, one is already very close to what might be termed the "legitimate" stock market. As an old saying goes, "there is no such thing as dirty money". It is easy enough to switch around legitimate and phoney investments, using both legally and illegally obtained money, thereby both acquiring wealth and "laundering" money from skimming the gaming tables, rackets, and so on.

This is not to say that the old style did not survive. The very fact that gambling was one of the keys to the system shows that old Mafia traditions continued. Indeed, one of the most interesting dramas was played out in Las Vegas.

THE RETURN TO LAS VEGAS

After "legitimate" business, in the shape of Howard Hughes, had failed to make significant profits from the Las Vegas casinos, the Mob apparently drifted back in during the 1970s. The Chicago Mafia, headed by Tony Accardo, was very much to the fore.

Accardo was a classic "Roaring Twenties" style mafioso. Although he was only 14 when Prohibition started, he made his name as an enforcer for Al Capone. His nickname, "Joe Batters", refers to one particularly messy hit where he beat the victim to death with a baseball bat. In 1929, when he was only 23, he was one of the triumvirate that ran the Chicago Mob while Capone was doing time. The other two were Jake "Greasy Thumb" Guzik and Frank "the Enforcer" Nitti. With Paul "the Waiter" Ricca (1897–1972),

Joe Batters built on the foundations that Johnny Torrio and Big Al had laid, extending Chicago's influence all through the country.

A landmark came in 1977, when at a big "sit-down" the Chicago Mob acquired rights to Las Vegas. Until then Las Vegas had been "open", meaning that no one Family or regional syndicate had to be consulted about what to do, but the *quid pro quo* of giving Las Vegas to Chicago was that New York could have Atlantic City.

As it turned out, it was a very poor trade. Las Vegas is a resort town, whose only climatic defect is sometimes excessive heat. Atlantic City looks like a movie-set for the aftermath of a nuclear war, and suffers from a climate that is often cold, wet and cloudy. It is true that Atlantic City is only a bus ride from New York, but then, Las Vegas is only a (long) bus ride from Los Angeles. For those who are prepared to fly to the destination of their choice, Las Vegas wins hands down.

BELOW
Tony Accardo, a.k.a. Joe Batters, who was instrumental in acquiring control of Las Vegas for the Chicago Mob in the 1970s. He is seen here leaving court in 1958, having been charged—as is traditional—with income tax evasion.

RIGHT
Scenes of Atlantic City and its casinos, which turned out to be a very poor exchange for Las Vegas for the New York Mob.

JOE BANANAS

By 1986, a substantial faction of the New York Mob was very unhappy about this, and under Joe Bonnano ("Joe Bananas") they decided to try to muscle in on Chicago's Las Vegas territory.

Joe Bananas was another old-timer, a year older than Joe Batters. The Banana War of 1964–69 used to be held up as the last of the old-style blood-on-the-streets gang wars, when Joe Bananas tried to whack out Carlo Gambino and Tommy Lucchese, heads of two other major New York crime Families. He failed, despite machine-gun killings and all the old trappings, but astonishingly he managed to stay alive: whether because of Commission policy or Commission inefficiency is a moot point.

Incredibly, though, the two Joes faced off in a big way in 1986 to 1988 in another gang war in Las Vegas. By this time, they were both in their eighties, as was Moe Dalitz. Moe was the highest-ranking casualty of the Las Vegas wars. He was

shot and badly wounded at the age of about 87 in 1986, and then finished off with poison a few days later in hospital when four bullet wounds looked to be insufficient to have killed him.

According to William F. Roemer, Jr., the Commission approved Joe Bananas' attempt to move in on Joe Batters, though for reasons that are unclear. Roemers's accounts are however impossibly romanticized and always parrot the old FBI myths, such as Meyer Lansky as the brains and bankroll behind everything and the idea that non-Italians are excluded from many Mafia sit-downs – a somewhat inconsistent pair of assertions. Roemer is also a master, or at least an enthusiastic user, of invented dialogue.

If the Commission did approve what Joe Bananas was doing, they must immediately have wished they had not, because there was soon blood on the streets of Las Vegas – a sight that does not help when it comes to building customer confidence. Not only that, Joe Bananas also proved as incompetent at taking over Las Vegas as at taking over New York, and by 1988 the last of the great gang wars (at the time of writing) was over.

There was however an interesting footnote to it all. Joe Batters was acquitted of the murder of Moe Dalitz, of RICO (Racketeer-Influenced and Corrupt Organization Act) crimes, of bombing the counting house of a New York-influenced casino, of gambling charges, and of much else, but he was the *only* defendant who was not found guilty of all charges against him. What was more, a great deal of the evidence that was seemingly too shaky to secure a conviction for Joe Batters was, however, admissible before the Nevada Gaming Control Commission. In particular, hearsay is not admissible in a court of law, but it may be admissible in front of an administrative board. The result of all this was a grand, official "house

cleaning" of casinos owned or influenced by the Chicago Mob, although it is by no means clear whether this was a genuine purge or whether it was largely ceremonial. After all, the mob was getting increasingly skilled in the use of front men. At the end of the trial, both Joe Batters and Joe Bananas (in their late eighties) were living a retired life in the "sun belt" – remarkable for two such traditional hoodlums.

Despite their genius, the old Joes were however living fossils. The era of the "Teflon Godfather", the man who might occasionally do a few months or even a couple of years in the slammer for the sake of appearances, was over. The main reason for this was a 1970 federal statute of distinctly dubious morality in an allegedly free society, the Racketeer-Influenced and Corrupt Practices Act or RICO.

BELOW
Tony Accardo, a.k.a. Joe Batters, about to testify before the Senate investigations subcommittee on his involvement in organized crime. Another nickname, "Big Tuna", is the reason for the fish head on his cane.

THE RICO ACT

RICO flies in the face of the Fifth Amendment, which states (among other things) "nor shall any person be subject for the same offence to be twice put in jeopardy of life or limb". The sophistry with which it destroys the Constitution is that any crime which is committed in the course of the operations of a criminal "enterprise" or "commission" is a crime twice over: once in its own right, and once as a part of the "enterprise" or "commission". There is no doubt that many of those convicted under RICO deserve to be punished; although there is considerable doubt as to whether the government is not "bending" the law in much the same way as the accused when it indicts them under RICO.

Regardless of constitutional niceties, RICO has been used to put away top mafiosi for long sentences ever since a Supreme Court decision gave the green light for a generous interpretation of the statute in 1981. In this context, "long" can be 30 or 40 years, which translates to actual time served of anything from about a decade upwards.

For someone like Joe Batters, a decade in prison would mean that he would almost certainly die there. A man in his mid-eighties could hardly be expected to bounce out of prison, full of vim and vigour in his mid- to late-nineties, and then enjoy the fruits of his illegal labours. It might be perfectly possible for a Mafia Boss to run his operation from prison for many years – Lucky Luciano certainly did it – but if he knew he was likely to die behind bars, a lot of the incentive would go out of it. Worse still, from the point of view of those on the outside, an old man might be tempted to "sing" in return for a reduced sentence and at least the chance of dying at home surrounded by his family.

By a simple Darwinist process, younger "Godfathers" became far more preferable, because they were men who could do 10 or even 15 years in prison, and still come out reasonably vigorous. The classic example of the younger generation was John Gotti.

"JOHNNY BOY" GOTTI

John Gotti was (and still is) a strange blend of the old and the new. Most often likened to Albert Anastasia, the ruthless killer who himself died under assassins' bullets in 1957, Gotti was born in 1940 and worked his way up through the Mafia by solid hard work. A quick survey of his career up to his emergence as the top Godfather of the 1980s is an edifying example of how a small-time punk who seemed not to be very bright – he was always

getting caught – could learn from his mistakes and make something of himself.

The fifth of a dozen children, Gotti was born to a family of Neapolitan origin in the Bronx. He dropped out of high school in 1956, and was first arrested (for disorderly conduct, after a gang fight) in May 1957; the charge was dismissed two months later. He was already hanging around with gangs at that time. In the same year, he was arrested for stealing copper, and was given probation in return for a plea of guilty. In 1959 he was arrested for unlawful assembly, a somewhat odd charge which actually meant that he was present when a gambling joint was raided. If that was not enough to break the terms of his probation, his arrest a few months later for disorderly conduct, and the resulting $200 fine, should have set off the alarm bells. As it was, when the unlawful assembly charge finally came up, he was given a 60-day, suspended sentence.

SMALL-TIME HOOD

The analogy with a weak parent is irresistible. Repeatedly, the State of New York had wagged its finger at John Gotti and told him that he was a naughty boy, but they did not actually punish him. In 1961 he was arrested for having an offensive weapon in his car – a billy-club – and in 1963 he actually went to jail for 20 days as a result of a burglary. To a tough young man like him, this was nothing. In 1965 he was arrested repeatedly for a variety of offences: petty larceny, breaking and entering, and possession of bookmaking records, among other things. This time, he spent several months in jail, but in November 1967 he was a leader in a Mafia-sponsored hijacking at JFK Airport. He seems to have got away with this, but on 1 December he tried again, and was arrested and bailed. Less than six months later, he was involved in yet another hijack, this time of a tractor-trailer rig. This would become known as the Velvet Touch Caper, after the bar where the police had tapped the phones.

For the December hijacking, he was sent to Lewisberg federal prison for what everyone expected would be about two-and-a-half year sentence. He entered the prison on 14 May, 1969 and in October of the same year he was returned to New York to face additional, state charges for substantially the same offence. In return for a guilty plea, the prosecution agreed that Gotti should serve no extra time. Some hold this up as an example of "fixing", but it is equally feasible that it was merely an escape from what amounted to double jeopardy. For real luck, though, Gotti

ABOVE
John Gotti, born in 1940, had become the leading mafioso by the 1980s through solid hard work and learning from his mistakes.

found that for once the Constitution of the United States actually was respected, and it protected an American citizen. From everyone else's point of view, it may have been too bad that the citizen it so capriciously protected was John Gotti, but the inescapable fact was that the police had used illegal wire-taps. The case in the Velvet Touch Caper fell rapidly apart.

An aside is in order here. America is justly proud of its Constitution, but every now and then, the Constitution has effects that nobody likes very much. This gives rise to three possibilities: one is to change the Constitution; the second is to accept that adhering slavishly to the Constitution sometimes produces anomalies, and to live with

them; the third, and incomparably the worst, is to "bend" the Constitution.

"Bending" the Constitution is incomparably the worst because it removes the rule of law, and substitutes the rule of expediency. As soon as expediency is placed above the law, regardless of the motive, those who plead it are placing themselves on the level of the criminals. They are saying, in effect, that "might is right".

It is unlikely that John Gotti spent much time pondering this, because he had other fish to fry. In particular, Lewisburg seems to have lived up to the classic reputation of prisons as being a university of crime. John Gotti, the small-time hood, was growing into John Gotti, Godfather.

CAPO GOTTI

After his release from Lewisberg, Gotti began to mastermind hijackings rather than participating in them. When Anniello "Neil" Dellacroce was sent down in late 1972, on the by now traditional charge of income tax invasion, "Johnny Boy" Gotti was acting Capo of Neil's patch and was sufficiently senior to be dealing with Carlo Gambino, head of the Gambino Family.

In early 1973, Carlo Gambino's 29-year-old nephew Emanuel was kidnapped and $350,000 was demanded for his return. His wife managed to scratch up $100,000, but Emanuel was shot in the head anyway.

The police caught two of the kidnappers, and Gotti knocked over the third in Snoope's Bar and Grill on Staten Island on 22 May, 1973. That is, the man he killed – 32-year-old Irish-American James McBratney – was believed by many to have been involved in the Gambino case. It is virtually certain that McBratney was also involved in other kidnappings of gang members. On 3 June, 1974, Gotti was arrested for the murder of McBratney.

About a year later, he plea-bargained the murder into attempted manslaughter. His argument was that McBratney had attacked a friend of his, and that he was merely coming to the friend's aid. This time, there was no constitutional defence for what happened. Gambino simply benefited from the cheapness in which life is held not only among criminals, but also by the American judicial system. He received a sentence of four years, of which he served just under two.

While "Johnny Boy" was inside, Carlo Gambino died at the age of 74. He was replaced by Big Paulie Castellano. Big Paulie was officially recognized as the new leader of the Gambino Family, at about the same time that Anniello "Neil" Dellacroce left prison after serving four years on income tax charges (or twice as long, for bilking the government, as Gotti got for killing another human being).

Gotti got out on 28 July, 1977. Shortly afterwards, he was reputedly "made" as a mafioso. "Making" a mafioso (also known as "straightening out" and "coming home") is a ritual that probably derives as much from books and movies as from

ABOVE
Paul Castellano, shown here leaving court in 1985, was the head of the Gambino family until his death, after which Gotti took over.

Sicilian tradition. Blood oaths and the like were certainly no part of the 1930s' Syndicate. Regardless of the symbolism of what happened, and indeed regardless of what actually happened, Gotti was now very much on the inside. He was 37 years old.

It was at around this time that he started showing signs of the intelligence for which he has since been praised. For example, he enforced the ban on drug dealing because it generated too much heat. He rarely carried a gun, and he advised his lieutenants to do the same. A gun was a tool to be taken out and used when you needed it, but carrying one at all times was risky. He was *really* consolidating his position.

Then, on 18 March, 1980, there occurred one of those events which show what power really is. Gotti's son Peter, aged 12, was riding a motorized mini-bike when he was struck and killed by a neighbour of the Gotti family. The official version is that he shot out from behind a dumpster, and that John Favara hit him when he was blinded by sunlight. It would have been a tragedy in any household, but one day John Favara just disappeared, never to return.

The tragedy aside, Gotti behaved very much as one might expect a successful mafioso to behave for the next four or five years. Despite increasing heat from a number of Federal and State agencies, who in some cases assisted Gotti by their interdepartmental rivalry and refusal to exchange information, he continued to build the business on the traditional Mafia foundations of prostitution, extortion, and labour rackets, with a healthy sideline in hijacking. Or at least, he was accused of doing so, but nothing was ever proved.

BELOW
John A. Gotti, son of John J. Gotti the Mafia Boss. When Gotti's son Peter was killed in a road accident, the driver of the car "disappeared" shortly afterwards.

THE
CASTELLANO
TAPES

The real changes came in 1985, some months after Paul Castellano had been indicted on RICO charges – charges that could have put him away for the rest of his life, even if he lived to be 90. Serious, major-league bugging accounted for much of the evidence against him, and from transcripts of the bugging tapes, many mafiosi had learned that Big Paulie was also Big Mouth. More and more mafiosi were sucked in to the case, including the by now mortally ill Neil Dellacroce and the far from unwell John Gotti.

The customary sparring and delays were immediately set in motion, and the case was not scheduled to come to trial until December 1985. On the very day when the Dellacroce-Gotti trial was scheduled to start, 2 December, Aniello Dellacroce died.

Big Paulie Castellano then made two fatal mistakes. First, he failed to show up to pay his respects to his dead Underboss. In a society based on Respect with a capital "R", this was not an intelligent move. Second, he appointed Thomas Bilotti as his new Underboss.

Two weeks later, Castellano and Bilotti were dead, each shot six times in the head and upper body outside Sparks Steak House in New York. Castellano's trademark cigar was still burning in the gutter, beside his shattered glasses. Gotti was the new Godfather, and he looked the part in his $1,800 suits and hand-made shoes. However, this could not ward off the RICO trial, which eventually started in August 1986.

It was a circus, and Gotti was the star. Superbly turned out, always ready with a wisecrack or a *bon mot,* he twisted the media around his little finger. From holding the door open for a female reporter ("I was always taught to hold the door for a lady") to arguing with the judge about where the defendants would be permitted to eat ("Why don't we just not eat? Why should we eat? We don't deserve to eat"), he was newsworthy; he was cool; he was street-smart. These qualities play better than honesty, intelligence, education and hard work, as Diana Giacalone for the prosecution was to find out. Gotti's lawyer, who in many countries

LIKE US

would have been at the severe risk of being struck off for his cavalier courtroom style, effectively put *her* on trial. His summing up was a masterpiece.

"You want to get John Gotti? Get some evidence on him . . . Find a witness. Do it the right way. The ends do not justify the means.

"The government is people. It's my government, it's John Gotti's government. It's your government. But it's people. People do things wrong. You are the only shield we have against abuse of power, against tyranny."

The jury finally delivered its verdict. John Gotti, famed for his sharp double-breasted suits, good looks and bonhomie, really was the closest thing to a godfather for the 1990s.

The sentence passed was life without parole, but Gotti can afford lawyers to appeal from the date of conviction to the crack of doom. They might even come up with something. But the government clearly wants Gotti out of the way for a long, long time.

Whether this will matter very much to the Gambino crime Family is another matter. In theory, the whole Family could just continue its day-to-day operations without a single, unifying "Godfather". In practice, trouble is likely to arise if there are disputes among the Gambini Capos on how to divide the spoils, or if the Gambinos start quarrelling with the other Mafia Families about who is entitled to what.

In the final analysis, mafiosi are very like the rest of us. Where they are unlike the rest is that the gap between "I want to" and "I will" is very much smaller. Time and again, we see a Mafia man who "goes for it" without thinking of the consequences.

The trouble is, this "go for it" mentality is what we are taught at school; and the imagery of sports is very much the imagery of organized crime. One team "slaughters" another; the coach exhorts his team to "Kill 'em". It is also the mentality of the corporate raider, and of the "Social Darwinist" politician who cuts welfare benefits because the poor do not deserve any better.

Mafiosi are also the epitome of the American Dream. With very few exceptions, they make it to the top from the very humblest of backgrounds. There is some strange psychological mechanism that allows us to admire their success, while carefully shutting our eyes to some of what that success means. Say the word "Godfather", and we think of the elegant suits, the beautiful girls, the flashy cars, the big wad of bills flashed in the restaurant. We do not think of the bodies crumpled in the gutter, of the widows and orphans, of the days spent in terror knowing that anywhere, at any time, someone may step in front of you and pump a few bullets into your head.

Or maybe we do think about that, but we never

ABOVE
John Gotti (right) and his attorney, shortly after the jury withdrew to consider their verdicts. Gotti seems to be joking about how long the jury will take to reach a verdict as he points at his wrist.

RIGHT AND ABOVE RIGHT
The funeral of a mafioso (Albert Anastasia) and a floodlit state prison. A few mobsters do live comfortably to an old age, but most end up in one of two ways: incarcerated in a prison or interred in the ground after a violent end.

see ourselves in the position of the underdog, the victim. In our fantasies, we are the Godfathers, the invincible hit-men, the fur-clad floozies. Either way, we are having problems with reality.

However you look at it, that must be the verdict on any book about organized crime. We just do not know enough about our subject. Ultimately, our own experiences and our own predilections will determine whether we believe in some monolithic structure, a General Motors of crime, or in a constantly shifting world of alliances and double-crossing. After studying the Mafia closer than most people, I believe that the second model is (and always has been) much closer to the truth. I also believe that the web of political corruption that entangles both gangsters and politicians is far more important than any "Mafia" or "Cosa Nostra" or "Commission". In these pages, I have tried to paint some of the picture as I have seen it. The final decision must rest with you.

INDEX

PICTURE CREDITS